Behind the Screen

with Windows XP and Microsoft Office 2003

by Steve Hayes

Any sufficiently advanced technology is indistinguishable from magic. Arthur C. Clarke

Second Print Edition, February 2012

Copyright © 2011-2012 by Stephen J Hayes

ISBN 978-1-4716-0003-6

All rights reserved. This book may not be reproduced in any form, in whole or in part, without written permission from the author. Please contact steve@honeylink.co.uk.

TRADEMARKS/REGISTERED TRADEMARKS
Computer hardware and software brand names mentioned in this book are protected by their respective trademarks and are acknowledged here.

*To my wife, partner and best friend Lynne
whose helplessness before the infernal machine
inspired this book*

Table of Contents

Preface..v
   Why this book?...v
   What word processor?...vi
   What spreadsheet?..vi
1 Introduction...1
   1.1 Taking it in..1
   1.2 Conventions..1
2 Behind the screen...3
   2.1 Bits, bytes, characters, numbers and data......................................5
   2.2 Kilo, Mega, Giga and Tera...5
   2.3 The computer..6
   2.4 Programs and Data..7
   2.5 Bugs...8
   2.6 Crashes and viruses...8
   2.7 RAM and Hard Disks...9
   2.8 The BIOS and booting..10
   2.9 Writing a program...10
   2.10 Operating Systems and Applications..11
   2.11 Updates...11
   2.12 The keyboard, mouse and display..12
   2.13 The USB thumbdrive and printer...12
3 Basics of Windows...14
   3.1 Clicking and dragging with the mouse or touchpad....................14
   3.2 Starting the Web Browser..14
   3.3 Managing program windows...18
   3.4 Installing Microsoft Office..20
   3.5 Turning the computer off..20
4 Basics of word processing..22
   4.1 Starting Word..22
   4.2 Typing, copying and pasting text...24
   4.3 Drop-down menus..27
   4.4 Making changes..28
   4.5 Finding and replacing..29
   4.6 Selecting...33
   4.7 Paragraphs, margins, indents and tabs......................................34
   4.8 Word Wrapping and Justification 37
   4.9 Styles, Typefaces and Fonts..39
   4.10 Symbols..44
   4.11 Non-printing characters..45
   4.12 Checking your spelling...48

- 4.13 Saving the document..50
- 4.14 Printing the document...51
- 4.15 Documents attached to an e-mail...............................53
- 5 Files and folders..55
  - 5.1 The hard disk..55
  - 5.2 Finding files and making folders.................................57
  - 5.3 Using a thumbdrive..59
  - 5.4 Moving files and creating shortcuts............................61
  - 5.5 Making backups..64
  - 5.6 The clipboard..66
- 6 Structuring a document..67
  - 6.1 Autocorrection..67
  - 6.2 Formatting individual characters.................................68
  - 6.3 Numbering and bullets..68
  - 6.4 Formatting paragraphs..70
  - 6.5 Numbering the chapters and sections.........................72
  - 6.6 Inserting a table..74
  - 6.7 Adding a table of contents..76
  - 6.8 Giving the document a title..77
  - 6.9 Adding a footer or header and fields..........................78
  - 6.10 Templates..79
- 7 Spreadsheets..82
  - 7.1 Starting Excel..82
  - 7.2 Using functions and inserting rows and columns......84
  - 7.3 Column widths and absolute references.....................86
  - 7.4 Calculations, currencies and merged cells..................88
  - 7.5 Saving the spreadsheet..91
  - 7.6 Using the spreadsheet..91
- 8 Charts and Sorting...92
  - 8.1 Making an x-y (scatter) chart.......................................93
  - 8.2 Date and time calculations..96
  - 8.3 Making a column chart..98
- 9 Graphics and Pages..101
  - 9.1 Pasting graphics and data from the spreadsheet......101
  - 9.2 Portrait, Landscape and paper size............................102
  - 9.3 Pasting a spreadsheet...104
  - 9.4 Inserting pictures..107
  - 9.5 Formulas..109
  - 9.6 Sizing and anchoring graphics....................................109
  - 9.7 Adjusting the embedded spreadsheet........................113
- 10 Drawing and Columns..115
  - 10.1 Setting up columns...115
  - 10.2 Making a logo..116

    10.3 Adding a text box 121
    10.4 Making a letterhead 123
11 Mail merge 124
    11.1 Making the address list 125
    11.2 Making a template letter 126
    11.3 Sending a form letter 128
    11.4 Printing Envelopes 132
    11.5 Printing Labels 134
12 Epilogue 136

Preface

- Are you just starting out with a computer that you'll use to write letters, reports and other documents? Maybe you haven't even bought the computer yet.

- Have you been using a computer with a word processor and perhaps a spreadsheet for some time but still find it intimidating and feel that you don't understand what it's doing?

If you fit either description, this book is meant for you. It isn't intended for experienced power-users of a word processor or spreadsheet although they may pick up some useful ideas.

Why this book?

If you've browsed in a bookshop, you'll have seen many vast tomes covering word processors and spreadsheets. This book aims to be different:

- It's much shorter, covering stuff you'll actually use.
- It covers basic skills you need to use your computer as well as how to use the word processor and spreadsheet.
- It leads you through a voyage of discovery: you learn by seeing what needs to be done and then doing it.
- It explains concepts and jargon and tries to give you a mental image of how things work. You'll remember how to do them, see how to do similar tasks and be better placed to figure it out when something you try to do goes wrong.
- It doesn't pretend that things always go as they should.
- Although it specifically covers Microsoft Office 2003, it tries to be general enough so that you can use other word processors and spreadsheets too.

Because it's very easy to become stymied and dispirited due to a trivial misunderstanding, each chapter works through an exercise step-by-step and early chapters do this in detail with many screenshots. Later chapters assume familiarity with basic operations such as finding something in a dialogue box.

Often there's a choice between doing something the fastest and most efficient way and doing it in a way that's easier to understand and remember. Except for things you'll do often, this book favours the way that's easier to remember.

The exercises are chosen to be as quick and easy as possible to follow while still illustrating concepts, pitfalls and the capabilities of Microsoft Office. Once you're familiar with Office, you'll make documents that are much nicer than the ones produced here.

What word processor?

The book covers use of the Microsoft Word word processor under Windows XP with some guidance for using Windows Vista. Word is part of Microsoft Office.

Microsoft Office costs real money: quite a bit for a version that's licensed for business use. LibreOffice and the very similar OpenOffice are free open-source equivalents and, for most uses, are perfectly adequate. There's a different version of this book which describes how to use LibreOffice. There are two main reasons you might prefer Word:

- It's widely used by businesses and knowing how to use it effectively can be an advantage in the job market.
- Although LibreOffice can save documents in the file format used by Word, there can be minor glitches when these files are opened in Word.

What spreadsheet?

This book covers the Excel spreadsheet which is also part of Microsoft Office.

LibreOffice includes the Calc spreadsheet and much of what's covered here applies to it too.

1 Introduction

1.1 Taking it in

It would be nice if a computer was something like a toaster and a four page instruction leaflet was all that was needed. Unfortunately it isn't like that...

It's not a good idea to read this book all the way through and try to learn everything in each chapter as you go along. You'll get overwhelmed. It's better to work through the exercises, just remembering the bits that seem immediately useful. After you start using them, skim through the chapters again. More of the details will seem relevant.

Perhaps do one chapter a day. You'll remember things better once you've slept on them.

Chapter 2 shows how your computer works and explains a lot of jargon. Chapters 3 and 5 show how to use Windows itself.

Chapter 4 covers the basics of word processing. The concepts and capabilities it describes apply to most word processors.

Chapter 6 covers useful features that even many experienced Word users seem unaware of. Chapters 7 and 8 cover Excel spreadsheets.

Chapters 9 to 11 cover more advanced word processing: chapter 9 mentions the Microsoft Equation formula editor and chapter 10 touches on the Word Picture program. You can skim these very quickly just to see what's there, then work through their exercises once you know that the material covered will be useful. If all you want to do is to write the occasional letter, this may be never.

Some versions of Microsoft Office include the Powerpoint presentation program and the Access database. This book doesn't cover those at all.

There is a comprehensive index.

1.2 Conventions

When an important term is introduced, it's shown in **bold**.

From Chapter 3 on, you'll be following through exercises on your computer. In some cases, you need to type in a specific phrase or look for a phrase in a dialogue box or drop-down menu. These are shown in italics, e.g. type *The quick brown fox jumps over the lazy dog.*

> *There are optional paragraphs formatted in italics like this one. They contain information that may be interesting, useful and helps you to understand the steps being described. You can safely skip over them if you want to. Come back and read them later.*

The steps are divided into sections. Each section introduces a few concepts. There's a list of these concepts at the end of the section entitled *What you learned*. Don't worry if you didn't learn all of them – just come back later.

Some of these concepts were only covered in the optional paragraphs. They're shown in italics too. If you skipped the optional paragraphs, you shouldn't worry about these concepts.

2 Behind the screen

The magical and powerful Wizard of Oz turned out to be someone very ordinary standing behind a curtain. Computers may be powerful but they ain't magical.

"I'm thinking of buying a computer. It has:

- **An Intel Dual Core 3.3GHz processor**
- **4GB of RAM**
- **A 500GB hard drive**
- **An Intel HD2000 Graphics adapter**
- **Windows 7"**

Sounds impressive but what does it all mean? Once you've read this chapter, you'll know. You'll also find it easier to understand why your computer behaves the way that it does.

Let's start with a machine from the age before computers.

Photo author: Dominic Alves, Brighton, England

This is a teleprinter machine. Like a typewriter, it has a keyboard and a printing mechanism but it can be connected to another similar machine, perhaps thousands of miles away. When the operator presses a key on the keyboard, the corresponding letter is printed on the distant machine. Before these machines were introduced, messages had to be sent by skilled operators using Morse code – teleprinters made things much easier.

On the left hand side of the machine are a roll of paper tape and mechanisms to punch and read it. We'll have a closer look at these because a modern computer uses an electronic equivalent of paper tape to store what you type into it.

When the paper tape punch is switched on and the operator presses a key, a row of holes is punched in the tape and it moves forward one row. A whole message can be saved on tape and stored. At any time, it can be fed back through the reader and the message printed out or sent to a distant teleprinter.

Here's a length of tape with the words *Paper Tape* punched into it. Each letter corresponds to a row of holes in the tape – a coded letter (though not a secret code). The letters *a*, *p* and *e* occur twice and the pattern of holes is the same both times. Also notice that a row was punched when the operator pressed the spacebar between the two words. When the tape is fed through the reader, this row doesn't print anything but, just like when the spacebar is pressed, it causes the printing position to move forward, leaving a blank space.

> *The tape, when bought new, already has the small holes. Each row that is punched can contain up to eight of the larger holes, three on the far side of the small hole and five on the near side. (It happens that the words Paper Tape don't cause any holes to be punched in the nearest position on the tape or in the position just this side of the small holes.)*

You could think about doing some clever things with paper tape.

- You could print the same message many times.
- You could make copies of the tape (the teleprinter itself can do this).
- You could post a copy to someone.
- You could cut up the tape and stick the pieces together to rearrange the words, sentences, etc.

These, of course, are things you can do with a word processor. It does them in much the same way as you could with paper tape, scissors and glue, even using the same codes for the keys pressed, but it does them much more quickly and easily because it keeps the codes in an electronic memory.

2.1 Bits, bytes, characters, numbers and data

At each row on the paper tape, you saw that there can be up to 8 holes. There are 256 (2^8) possible patterns of holes that could be punched in each row (including no holes at all).

Each place that a hole could be represents one binary digit or **bit** of data. If a hole is present, we say it's a binary 1. If it's absent, we say it's a binary zero.

Instead of the presence or absence of a hole, a bit can be represented by an electrical voltage or current – one value represents a zero, a different value represents a 1.

We refer to 8 bits as a **byte** and, as noted above, a byte can have any of 256 possible values. A selection of these can be used to represent various **characters** – the 26 capital letters (*A-Z*), the 26 lower case ones (*a-z*), the digits *0-9*, the various punctuation symbols, space and other functions such as RETURN (new line). The commonest selection is the ASCII (*American Standards Committee for Information Interchange*) code used by the teleprinter machine above.

Or a byte can represent a number in the range 0 to 255 (or perhaps -128 to +127). Two bytes taken together (16 bits) can represent numbers in the range 0 to 65,535 (0 to $2^{16}-1$). Four bytes (32 bits) can represent numbers in the range 0 to 4,294,967,295.

> *Binary numbers of various lengths can be written out (should you ever need to) as a series of ones and zeroes but, if they are long, that quickly gets confusing. It's common to put the bits in groups of four (giving 16 possible values) and represent each group as a number 0-9 or letter A-F. This is hexadecimal notation.*

The term **data** just means information that is stored or transmitted.

2.2 Kilo, Mega, Giga and Tera

In conventional language, **kilo** is 1000, **mega** is 1 million, **giga** is 1000 million (usually called a billion) and **tera** is a million million (1000 billion). For example, a kilometre is 1000 metres.

In some situations with computers (which are pointed out later), different values are used. Kilo can be 2^{10} (1,024), mega can be 2^{20} (1,048,576) and giga can be 2^{30} (1,073,741,824).

2.3 The computer

As this diagram shows, the main unit of a typical desktop computer contains (among other things) memory devices, a CPU, a hard disk drive (perhaps more than one) and a graphics adaptor. The memory and CPU are plugged into a large printed circuit board (the **motherboard**). The graphics adaptor may be part of the motherboard or it may be a separate plug-in card.

A display screen (monitor), mouse and keyboard are connected to the main unit. With a laptop, the screen and keyboard are built into the main unit along with, usually, a touchpad in place of the mouse.

The **CPU (Central Processing Unit)** is the heart of the computer. It's a microchip containing complex electronic logic circuits, usually made by Intel (e.g. Pentium) or AMD (e.g. Athlon).

The **memory** is like a huge array of pigeon-holes, each able to hold one byte of data (making each one equivalent to a row on a paper tape). A number is sent from the CPU to the memory over the address bus to select a particular pigeon-hole. The address bus might consist of 32 separate electrical paths on the motherboard – these could select any of 4,294,967,296 pigeon-holes although they may not all exist.

> *Because of the way the addresses work, computer memories have a size which is a power of two. For this reason, their sizes are quoted using the alternative definitions of kilo, mega and giga mentioned previously. For example, a 1 GB (gigabyte) memory can store 1,073,741,824 bytes.*

When the CPU needs to store or retrieve a byte, it uses the address bus to select the required location (pigeon-hole). If it's storing a byte there, it drives the data bus (consisting of eight separate electrical paths) to the voltages representing the byte it wants to store. If it's retrieving a byte, the memory drives the data bus and the CPU looks at the voltages to see what is stored in that pigeon-hole.

> *There's some simplification here. To speed things up, modern computers have 32 or 64 paths in the data bus and can access 4 or 8 successive bytes at the same time.*

2.4 Programs and Data

As you saw, bytes stored in the memory can represent characters or numbers, but they can also represent instructions for the CPU. When the computer first starts up, the CPU reads successive bytes from the memory starting at a fixed location and performs the operations that they specify. For example, an instruction might say to add numbers from two different locations in memory and store the result in a third location. Another instruction might say to compare characters from two locations in memory and, if they match, start fetching instructions from a different location instead of the usual next one.

Although each instruction only specifies a simple operation, a long sequence of them can do something apparently very complex and sophisticated. A modern computer can carry out billions of instructions every second.

A sequence of instructions makes up a program. Your word processor is a program with millions of instructions. Some of them need to be carried out many times over to accomplish even an apparently trivial task such as showing a letter on the screen.

We'll refer to instructions for the CPU stored in the memory as **Programs** and everything else (for example, word-processor documents) as **Data**.

When the CPU is following instructions for a program, we say that the program is **running** or **executing** (they mean the same thing).

2.5 Bugs

When a program contains millions of instructions, it inevitably has some logic errors. An error in a program is often referred to as a **bug**. Major bugs are spotted and fixed quite quickly but ones that are only seen intermittently or under unusual circumstances can persist for years before a programmer tracks down what's causing the problem and fixes it.

> *The expression originated when an early computer malfunctioned because of a moth trapped in one of its relays.*

2.6 Crashes and viruses

You're probably wondering how the CPU knows which parts of the memory contain programs and which contain data. The answer is that, in general, it doesn't know. Programs are designed so that, after the CPU processes each instruction, it gets another instruction, not some other piece of data.

Sometimes this goes wrong and the CPU starts treating data as instructions. This rarely causes anything interesting to happen. Sometimes the computer just freezes up. Other times, it detects that there's a problem and either stops the faulty program or stops entirely with an error message (a **crash**). The message may include long numbers in the hexadecimal notation described earlier – only the programmer can make sense of these.

Because of flaws in some of the programs on the computer, malicious people can use various tricks to get it to start running a program that shouldn't be there. This is a computer virus.

> *Strictly speaking, the correct term for all programs like this is **malware**. A virus is malware of a particular type.*

> *An attack often starts when your computer opens something on a page of a dubious website or something attached to a spam e-mail.*

Once an attacker has got one malware program onto a computer, they can use it to install more programs whenever they like. It's common for them to install a program that uses your computer and internet connection to send vast numbers of spam e-mails. They can also use it and thousands like it to overload commercial websites, holding them to ransom.

*A **keylogger** is a very nasty form of malware. It records every key that you press and sends the information over the internet to an attacker. For example, they can see your passwords. That's why most banks require you to click things on the screen to log in – it's much harder to capture that.*

*Attackers mainly target Windows systems although other systems aren't immune. You can buy **anti-virus** programs that try to detect any malware on your computer and block or remove it. Unfortunately anti-virus programs always slow the computer down and some well-known ones can make it intolerably slow.*

A new Windows computer often comes with a trial version of an anti-virus program. Usually, this starts demanding that you subscribe to a paid-for service after 30 days or so.

For home use or in a small business with up to 10 PCs, you can remove the trial program and download and install the free Microsoft Security Essentials from windows.microsoft.com/mse.

2.7 RAM and Hard Disks

Most of the memory in the computer is RAM. This stands for Random Access Memory – the name goes back to the earliest computers and isn't particularly meaningful for us. What's significant is that data stored in RAM is lost when the computer shuts down. Copies of programs and important data such as your word-processed documents need to be kept on the hard disk. Some people think of the disk as being part of the computer's memory but we'll view it as something separate.

The hard disk contains a number of spinning disks which have a coating similar to that used on recording tapes. Magnetic heads can record data as a series of magnetised regions on the coating, then play them back and recover the data. The magnetised data remains when power is off and the disk can hold much more data than would fit into an affordable amount of RAM. However, the CPU needs to use a program to write data to and fetch it from the hard disk and this is perhaps a million times slower than saving it in and getting it from RAM.

> *Because the disk is not addressed in the same way as the RAM, 1GB of hard disk space usually means 1,000,000,000 bytes (the conventional meaning of giga) rather than the 1,073,741,824 bytes that 1 GB of RAM could hold.*

2.8 The BIOS and booting

Now here's a puzzle. If the CPU needs a special program to get data from the disk and any program in RAM is lost when the computer is shut down, how can it start up again? The answer is the **BIOS** memory. This is a different type of memory known as ROM (Read Only Memory). Data in the ROM is loaded at the factory and is permanent (often a Flash memory is used instead which you can reprogram but that's a complex and risky process). When the computer starts, the CPU begins fetching instructions at a fixed location in the BIOS memory where there's a program that can access the hard disk, copy further programs from it into the RAM and start them. This is the **boot** process – a term inspired by the image of the computer lifting itself by its own bootstraps.

The BIOS allows various options to be set when the computer starts up – you need to hold down a particular key or combination of keys when the computer starts to get to the options. For example, the BIOS can be set to load a program from a DVD or thumbdrive instead of the hard disk when the computer starts. This is the way that programs such as the Windows operating system are installed on (copied to) a new computer.

2.9 Writing a program

> *This is far beyond the scope of this book but a quick overview might be interesting.*

A program as stored on the hard disk or in RAM may make sense to the CPU but it makes no sense to you or me – it's just a series of meaningless bytes.

Programs are written in a more user-friendly language using a program quite like a word-processor. The new program (known as **source code**) is translated to instructions understood by the CPU using another program known as a compiler.

Examples of programming languages are Basic, C, C++, C#, Cobol, Fortran, Java, Perl and Python. There are many more, rather more than we really need.

2.10 Operating Systems and Applications

The **operating system** consists of the program that's loaded from the hard disk and started by the BIOS plus a large collection of additional programs that can be started and used to do basic computing tasks such as maintaining data on the hard disk. We'll see some of these programs later on. Examples of operating systems are the various versions of Microsoft Windows, Apple's OS-X and open-source Linux systems such as Ubuntu.

> **Open-source** means that the source code of the program is published freely and anyone who wants to can improve it. Open-source programs, including LibreOffice and versions of Linux are normally available at no cost.

Applications (or **apps**) are programs which aren't part of the operating system itself although sometimes they may be included with it. Most Linux versions automatically include LibreOffice or OpenOffice as a word processor and spreadsheet. Windows includes a very basic word processor – WordPad.

Microsoft Office is an application not included in Windows itself – it must be paid for and installed separately.

> *Smartphones are also little computers with an operating system (e.g. Android – derived from Linux) and apps.*

2.11 Updates

A Windows computer that has an internet connection periodically checks with Microsoft to see if any of its operating system programs can be replaced with newer versions where bugs have been fixed. This is particularly important if the bugs are making the computer vulnerable to malware. If an update is needed, the computer automatically downloads the new programs and installs them. Unfortunately, it usually needs to be restarted afterwards.

Individual application programs may also check to see if they need updating.

Some other operating systems handle updates much better than Windows.

2.12 The keyboard, mouse and display

Programs running on the CPU need to be able to tell which keys are pressed on the keyboard and when and where the mouse is moved. We don't need to examine how this is done.

Programs also need to control the display. The display itself is like a television – it needs a continuous signal. The Graphics Adaptor creates this signal. The program only sends instructions to the adaptor when it needs to make changes to the display.

Modern graphics adaptors can be very powerful. This lets the program create complex images by sending relatively simple and quick instructions to the adaptor. This is a big advantage for game programs but even the simplest graphics adaptor is sufficient for web browsing, word processing and other office-type programs.

2.13 The USB thumbdrive and printer

You'll want to connect a printer to your computer so that you can print out your documents. You may also have a USB thumbdrive / Data Stick available so that you can save copies of your documents and move them to a different computer. Even the smallest and cheapest thumbdrive sold now will be adequate for this.

We can now return to the question at the start of this chapter: what does all the gobbledegook about that computer mean:

- An Intel Dual Core 3.3GHz processor. This is the CPU microchip. It runs at 3.3 Gigahertz (3,300,000,000 steps per second) and has two CPUs internally so it can do two operations simultaneously.
- 4GB of RAM. 4 Gigabytes of RAM can store 4,294,967,296 bytes, equivalent to nearly 7000 miles of paper tape. It can hold many programs and other data at the same time. They won't need to be copied to and from the hard disk as often which speeds things up.

- A 500GB hard drive. The hard disk could theoretically hold 500,000,000,000 bytes, equivalent to nearly 800,000 miles of paper tape
- An Intel HD2000 Graphics adapter – you might want something better if you plan to play computer action games.
- Windows 7 – Microsoft's current version.

This would be a good computer for demanding tasks such as video editing. If all you want to do is word processing, spreadsheets, e-mail and web-browsing, any modern computer will be more than adequate and you could save some money.

> *In the early days of personal computers, Bill Gates remarked that 640 KB of RAM was all that anyone would ever need. A modern* **PC (Personal Computer)** *has thousands of times more RAM but Windows still manages to fill it up.*

3 Basics of Windows.

This chapter covers basics such as how to start and close programs, manage their windows and switch between them. Maybe you already know this.

3.1 Clicking and dragging with the mouse or touchpad

When you move the mouse or drag your finger over the touchpad, you'll see a **cursor** move on the screen. This is the **mouse cursor** – it may be an arrow, a hand or I-shaped and may change as it moves about. When we talk of **clicking** somewhere or on something, this means moving the cursor to that place on the screen, then pressing the left hand button on the mouse briefly.

Instead of using the left mouse button, you can click with the right hand one. This is **right-clicking** and usually has a different effect from normal clicking.

Clicking the left mouse button twice in quick succession is called **double-clicking**. If you click too slowly, the computer sees your clicks as two normal ones – double clicking has a different effect from this. Sometimes, you need to click three or four times in quick succession: **triple-clicking** or **quadruple-clicking**.

If you keep the left hand button held down and move the cursor, this is called **dragging**. It can be used to move various things around on the screen. They end up in the position that they are when you release the button.

> *It's possible to change settings on the computer so that the mouse buttons are switched. This may suit left-handed people better. With that setting, clicking and dragging uses the right button and right-clicking uses the left button.*

3.2 Starting the Web Browser

> *Although this book doesn't cover using the web in any depth, it's something you're likely to want to do. This section gets you started but, more importantly, it shows you how to start a program and some of the things to look for in its window.*

Click on ![start] at the bottom left of the screen. A box appears.

If you're using Vista, the start button is in the same place but it looks different (![]).

*This is a **screenshot**. It's been changed to add candy stripe markings around important things and to blur out irrelevant ones. Section 9.4 shows how you can add screenshots to your documents.*

You'll usually see your choice of web browser program as circled at the middle left. If this is Microsoft Internet Explorer as shown here,

3.2 Starting the Web Browser   15

you can just click on it.

> *Instead, it might be an alternative browser such as Firefox or Chrome. These do the same job but will look a bit different from the screenshot below.*

> *If you want Internet Explorer, move the mouse pointer over All Programs (circled at bottom left). A list of programs appears as shown here. Click on Internet Explorer in the list (circled at middle right).*

The computer copies the Internet Explorer program from the hard disk into its RAM and starts running it. A **window** appears on the screen. Here it is if you're using Windows XP: it'll be slightly different if you're using another version of Windows.

At the top of the window is the **titlebar** showing the name of the program and the document or web site that is open.

> *In this case it's the Google search page. Google (www.google.com) is the best known and most popular* **search engine.**

> *Your web browser might start up with a different or blank page. Don't worry.*

Near the top left of the Internet Explorer window is a box where you can type the address of a web page. It's circled in the picture above.

Click in the box. All the text in it changes colour – it's highlighted. If this doesn't work, try double or triple-clicking. Type *www.bing.com*. This automatically replaces the highlighted text. Press RETURN (the large key at the right side of the keyboard with a left-facing arrow – it may also say ENTER). The Bing search page loads into Internet Explorer.

> Bing is Microsoft's equivalent to Google (even though you're using Windows, you can use any search engine you want). Both Google and Bing search pages feature a box where you can type a question or just some words, then press RETURN. A list of web pages found on the Internet is shown and you can click on the underlined **link** for any of them to view it. In general, these pages aren't controlled by either Google or Bing: there's no guarantee of their quality, truthfulness or freedom from malware.
>
> When you click on a link on any web page, the address in the circled box changes to that of the new page. If you already know the address of a web page, you can just type it directly into the box and press RETURN.
>
> You can return to pages you were viewing previously by clicking ⬅ (circled). Further details of using the web are outside the scope of this book.
>
> This book shows the names of keys on the keyboard in capitals. BACKSPACE is usually a large key above RETURN with a left-pointing arrow. The wide SPACEBAR is below the letter keys. ALT is to its left. TAB is near the top left: it may be marked with arrows pointing to left and right. ESC (Escape) should be at the top left. DELETE (or DEL) should be somewhere near the right hand side of the keyboard. There may be CTRL (Control) and SHIFT keys on both sides of the SPACEBAR: you can use the one on either side, whichever is more convenient. The SHIFT keys may only be marked with upward pointing arrows.
>
> There are also four keys close together near the right-hand side of the keyboard that are marked with arrows pointing up, down, left and right. These are referred to as the **arrow keys**.

At the right hand end of the titlebar are three on-screen **buttons** (circled). Clicking ☒ would close (end) the program – don't click it now.

What you learned:

- **How to start your web browser.**
- **What a window is.**
- **Where the window titlebar is and what it shows.**
- **How to go to a web site by typing in its address.**
- *How to quickly return to a web page you viewed previously.*
- *Where various keys are on the keyboard.*
- *How to use a search engine such as Google or Bing.*

3.3 Managing program windows

Click on ▬ (one of the three circled buttons). The web browser window disappears but, if you look at the **taskbar** at the bottom of the screen, you can see the name of the web page. The browser is still running but has been **minimised**. Thanks to a technique called **multi-tasking**, other programs can run at the same time – if you want to, you can start another one (e.g. an e-mail program) now. Each program that's running appears on the taskbar and you can switch to it by clicking on its name.

*When no programs are running or all of them are minimised, most of the screen is occupied by the **desktop**. It may have icons on it: you'll be adding more in Section 5.4.*

If you click on the name of a program that isn't minimised but is partly or completely hidden by another window, its window is brought to the front. If its window was at the front, clicking the name on the taskbar will minimise it. If you can't see the window for your program, try clicking its name on the taskbar again.

Go back to the web browser window. If the third button is showing a single square (□), click on it. The window fills the screen and the button now shows two squares (🗗). This **maximised** the window. You'll usually want the window for your word processor or spreadsheet to be like this so you can see as much as possible of your document unless you're working with another program or document at the same time.

Click on 🗗. It now shows a single square and the window will probably become smaller.

The markings on the two buttons show what will happen if you click them. The single line looks like a program that's minimised and only visible on the taskbar. The single square looks like a program that's maximised and filling the screen. The two squares represent your program and perhaps another one (or several other programs) visible at the same time.

Place the cursor at the bottom right corner of the Internet Explorer window. It should change to a double-ended arrow. Hold down the left mouse/trackpad button then, keeping it held down, drag the corner so that the window becomes smaller or larger. This is **resizing**: the window stays at the new size when you release the button.

You can place the cursor over any corner or side of the window and, while it's a double-ended arrow, you can drag that corner or side to change the size and shape of the window. Make sure for now that it isn't filling the whole screen.

Now place the cursor over the titlebar at the top of the window away from the three buttons. Hold down the left mouse button and move the cursor. The window is dragged. Release the button: the window stays at its new position.

By adjusting the size and position of their windows, you can see and use more than one program at the same time.

The web page may not all fit in the window. If so, scroll bars appear at the right hand and bottom of the window. These are marked with arrows in the previous picture. If the window on your computer doesn't have these scroll bars, make it smaller until they appear.

The scroll bar at the right side lets you move the web page up and down in the window by clicking on the arrows at each end, by dragging the large button between them up and down or by clicking on the area below (or above) the large button. Experiment with it.

The scroll bar at the bottom works the same way. It lets you move the web page from side to side in the window.

Other programs including Word and Excel have windows that work the same way as the web browser one. They also have the titlebar, the three buttons and they may have scrollbars.

You can close the Internet Explorer window by clicking on its ☒. If you started any other programs, close them the same way. The programs stop running and the RAM they were using is freed.

What you learned:

- How to minimise a window.
- How to maximise a window.
- How to resize and move windows.
- What scrollbars do and how to use them.
- What the taskbar does and where it is.
- How to run more than one program at a time and switch between them.
- How to close (stop) a program.

3.4 Installing Microsoft Office

With luck, Microsoft Office will already be installed on your computer. If it's only a trial version, you'll need to get out your credit card within a month after you start using it and make a payment to Microsoft to unlock it.

You can download Office 2010 from the *office.microsoft.com* website or buy it on a DVD from a computer store. However, this isn't the appropriate version of this book if you're planning to use Office 2010.

If you have Office 2003 on a DVD or CD, you can install it to your computer by inserting the disk and following the instructions that appear on the screen. You'll probably need to enter an installation key from a sticker in the packaging. Remember that, if the disk is a copy or if it's already been used to install Office on a different computer, you might not be licensed to install another copy on your computer.

Even if Microsoft Office is already installed and unlocked, its version may not be licensed for business use.

> *Why not avoid all these hassles? You can legally download, install and use LibreOffice instead of Microsoft Office at zero cost. There's a different version of this book that covers installing and using LibreOffice on Windows XP.*
>
> *If it's all too complicated, get a friend to sort out your installation. It only needs to be done once.*

3.5 Turning the computer off

When you've finished using the computer you should turn it off correctly so that all documents, settings, etc. are saved.

Click [start], then click [O] (circled in the Section 3.2 screenshot). A box appears in the middle of the screen offering several choices:

- Click [O] (**Turn Off**) to shut the computer down completely. Next time you start it up, you'll have to wait while it goes through the boot-up process. Then you'll have to reopen any documents you were working on.

- Click [ ] (**Stand By**) to shut down the CPU and most other parts of the computer, keeping programs and open documents in the RAM. When you start the computer again, it's ready to use in a few seconds but, until then, it continues drawing a small amount of power (e.g. from its battery if it's a laptop) to keep the RAM working. If power is lost or the battery runs down, you could lose recent changes to the documents. It's wise to save them before putting the computer in Stand By.

- When you move the mouse cursor over [ ], you may see a message to press SHIFT and click to **Hibernate**. This is like Stand By but Hibernate saves data in the RAM to a special part of the hard disk so the computer can fully power down. It's a bit slower to start up again than with Stand By but still much quicker than if you turned the computer off completely.

- Clicking [ ] (**Restart**) shuts the computer down, then reboots it immediately. You can use this if the computer is behaving strangely and you think restarting it might help.

What you learned:

- **How to turn off the computer correctly and why you should always do this.**
- *How to Stand By, Hibernate or Restart the computer and what these do.*

4 Basics of word processing

This chapter shows how to type text into a new document, make changes to it, do some basic formatting, save the document on the hard disk and print it. You'll also learn some important concepts, terms and techniques.

> *Although you're using an older version of Microsoft Word, most of the steps covered in this chapter are similar for other word processor programs. Word 2010 replaces the drop-down menus with the "ribbon" interface. It has the same functions in a different format.*
>
> *The document made in this chapter will be used again in Chapter 10.*

4.1 Starting Word

Click on [start], then move the mouse pointer over *All Programs* (circled below). A list appears. Move the mouse pointer over *Microsoft Office* in the list. Another list appears. Move the mouse pointer over *Microsoft Office Word* and click.

> *Alternatively, you can click on New Office Document (also circled below), click on the General tab, click on Blank Document, then click [OK].*

22

You've copied the Word program from the hard disk into RAM. There may be a few seconds delay before it starts running and a window appears on the screen. Here it is if you're using Windows XP. It will be slightly different if you're using another version of Windows.

4.1 Starting Word   23

> *Once you've used Word a few times, Windows may add it to the list of programs above All Programs that appears when you click* **start** *. Once it's in that list, you can start it quickly by clicking on it there.*

There's all or part of a white page on a grey background in the Word window below the ruler. The page may be too large or too small to see comfortably. The circled box near the top controls the **zoom** factor: the ratio between the size of things on paper and on the screen. You can click ▼, then click to select a different factor from the drop-down list that appears: a lower number means you can see more of the page but things on it may be too small to see clearly.

> *The zoom ratio is only approximate: it depends on the size and resolution of your computer's screen.*

To the right of the document there may or may not be be a multi-function **task pane** marked *a* above. It's showing links to on-line help functions here. Sometimes it has other functions which you'll see later such as letting you format paragraphs. If it's in the way, you can close it and see more of your document by clicking on the circled ✗. It'll reappear when you try to do something that needs it.

What you learned:

- **How to start Word.**
- **How to change the size of the page on the screen by zooming.**
- **What the task pane does and how to get rid of it.**

4.2 Typing, copying and pasting text

Click anywhere on the blank page. There should be a flashing vertical line near the top left. This is the **text cursor** which shows where anything you type will go.

Type *The quick brown fox jumps over the lazy dog. X.* We'll be referring to a sequence of letters like this as **text**.

> *The text is stored as a series of bytes in your computer's RAM. If you pulled out the computer's power plug now (don't try it), it would be lost.*

Move the mouse cursor to just before the X that you just typed. Hold down the left mouse button and drag the cursor leftwards to the start of the word *The*. The text you dragged the cursor over is highlighted: it's shown as white on black. The **highlighting** shows that it's **selected**.

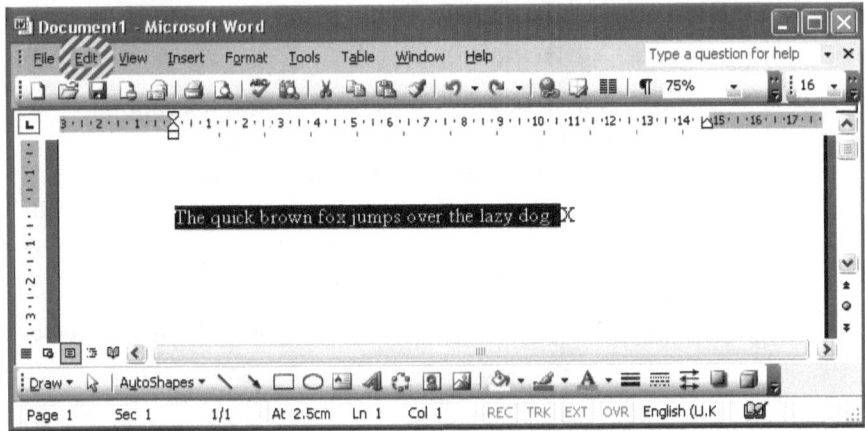

Click on *Edit* (circled), then on *Copy* in the drop-down menu that appears.

> *Microsoft Office programs, including Word, don't show items that you haven't used recently in drop-down menus. If you don't see the item you want (Copy in this case), click ⮟ at the bottom of the menu. More items appear.*

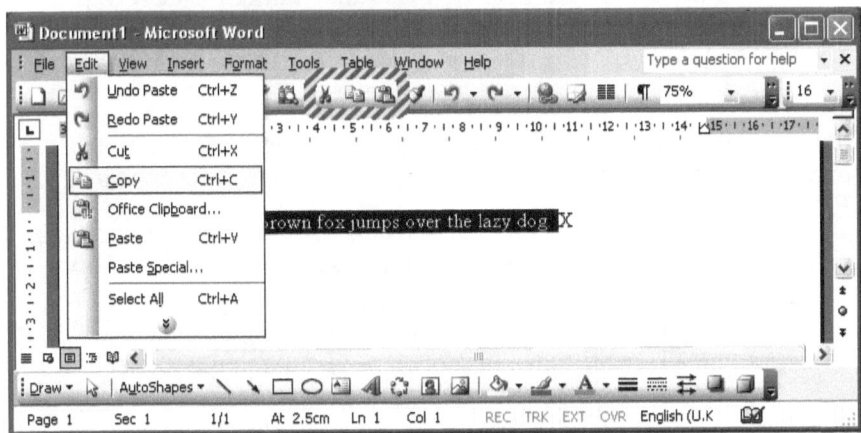

This copies the highlighted text to the **clipboard**.

> *Imagine making a copy of a paper tape containing the highlighted words.*

Notice *Ctrl+C* next to the word *Copy*. This is a **keyboard shortcut**. Pressing these keys together does the same as going to the drop-down

4.2 Typing, copying and pasting text   25

Edit menu and clicking on *Copy*. *Ctrl+V* is shown next to the word *Paste*.

You can use that keyboard shortcut now to save time. Hold down the CTRL key and press *V* five times.

> *The first time you press CTRL+V, it removes the highlighted text, puts a copy of the text on the clipboard in its place and places the text cursor at the end of it. In this case, the text was replaced with a copy of itself but the highlighting was removed. You could do the same thing by moving the mouse cursor to the end of the highlighted text and clicking.*
>
> *The next four times you press CTRL+V, another copy is inserted at the cursor position.*
>
> *Underneath the list of drop-down menus (e.g. Edit) is a **toolbar** containing **icons**. You may see some or all of the three that are circled above.*
>
> *Instead of using the Edit menu or the keyboard shortcuts, you can click on* 🗐 *to copy highlighted text to the clipboard and click on* 📋 *to paste the text.*
>
> *There are often several ways to do something. It's easy to find something in a drop-down menu but quicker to click on a toolbar icon such as* 🗐 *and even quicker to use a keyboard shortcut if you remember what it is.*

Release the CTRL key. The text cursor should be after the pasted sentences and just in front of the *X*. Press DELETE. *X* disappears.

> *Word has a feature called Intellisense which tries to anticipate what you want to do and make it easier. Unfortunately it often does exactly the opposite. In this case, if you try to select the sentence and space without having something unselected after it (i.e. the X), Intellisense insists on putting each pasted sentence in a separate paragraph.*

Press RETURN twice. The text cursor moves down. Type *What do these dogs like?*.

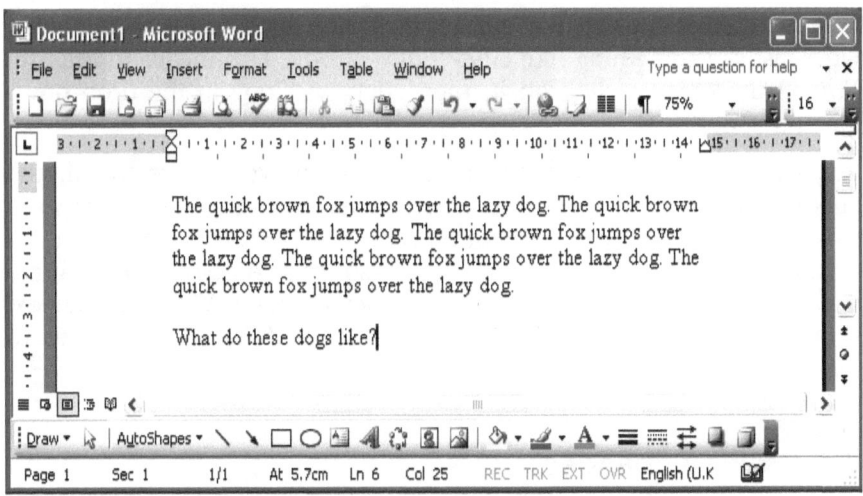

Why is this document such drivel? It's so you don't have to spend much time typing it in and you won't be distracted thinking about what it says and how you could improve it.

What you learned:

- **How to start typing a document.**
- **How to select (highlight) text by dragging with the mouse.**
- **How to use a drop-down menu.**
- **How to copy selected text to the clipboard.**
- **What keyboard shortcuts are.**
- **What** *Press CTRL+V* **means.**
- **How to paste text from the clipboard.**
- *What a toolbar is.*
- *What an icon is.*
- *That any existing highlighted text is replaced with pasted text.*
- *What Intellisense is and that it can be annoying.*
- *That there are often several ways to do something.*

4.3 Drop-down menus

You saw how, when you click on *Edit*, a drop-down menu appears and you can choose a particular editing operation such as *Copy*. In future, we'll just say something like *Click Edit > Copy*. This means to look for *Edit* in the menus, click on it, then click on *Copy* in the drop down menu that appears.

Sometimes additional submenus appear when you move the mouse cursor over an item in a drop down menu. For example, if you see *Click Insert > AutoText > Attention Line > ATTN:*, this means to click on the *Insert* menu, move the mouse cursor over *AutoText*, over *Attention Line* in the submenu that appears, then click on *ATTN:* in the next submenu. You can try this, then press BACKSPACE five times to remove *ATTN:*.

4.4 Making changes

You saw that a flashing cursor (a vertical line) appears at the position where anything you type will be placed. This is the **text cursor**.

You can place it by moving the mouse cursor to the position you want and clicking. Try this to place the flashing cursor after the word *jumps* in the first sentence.

You can also use the four arrow keys (Section 3.2) to move the flashing text cursor. Press the one pointing to the right several times to move the cursor past the word *over*.

Press DELETE three times. Each time you press the key, Word removes one letter from your document and moves all the ones after it back one place. You could imagine snipping a row of holes out of a paper tape and gluing it back together but the computer does this so quickly it seems instantaneous.

You should have got rid of the word *the* but you might have got rid of a space and the *t* and *h* instead so that you see the word *overe*. It depends whether you started with the cursor before or after the space. If the *e* is still there, press DELETE again to get rid of it, then press SPACEBAR to restore the space that you accidentally deleted.

Type *some*. Word inserts the word *some* into the document at the position of the cursor.

> You can add text to your document any time you want to. Just put the text cursor where you want it to go and start typing.
>
> Somewhere near the right side of the keyboard is a key labelled INSERT. Pressing this switches between **Insert** and **Overwrite**

mode. In overwrite mode, anything you type replaces the next letter rather than inserting what you type before it. If you find this is happening, look for INSERT. Maybe you accidentally pressed it. Just press it again.

You changed a word in the first sentence but it's still wrong. Press BACKSPACE four times. Just like DELETE, it deletes a letter each time you press it but it's the letter before the text cursor instead of the one after it.

Type *a*. Now the sentence is what you want: *The quick brown fox jumps over a lazy dog.*

What you learned:

- **How to reposition the text (flashing) cursor with the mouse.**
- **How to move the text cursor using the arrow keys.**
- **The computer inserts and deletes letters at the position of the text cursor.**
- **BACKSPACE deletes the letter before the text cursor.**
- **DELETE deletes the letter after the text cursor.**
- **You can accidentally switch to overwrite mode. Pressing INSERT fixes this.**

4.5 Finding and replacing

You changed the first sentence to read *a lazy dog*. You could change the next four sentences the same way but computers are supposed to make things easier.

Move the mouse cursor (not the flashing text cursor) over the offending *the* in the second sentence and double-click. The word becomes highlighted (its background colour changes). Double-clicking automatically selects a whole word.

Click *Edit > Replace....* A dialogue box appears (as shown later on).

Remember, this means to click to open the Edit drop-down menu, then click on Replace....

*A **dialogue box** is a small to medium sized window that appears when you're doing certain things. It shows information and may*

> *allow you to make various choices before clicking on a button to continue what you're doing.*

In *Find what:* in the dialogue box, the word *the* is highlighted – that's the text that it's ready to look for. If you wanted, you could type something different or edit the text.

Click [More ▼]. Additional options appear. Click on the tickbox next to *Match case* (circled below) so that a tick appears as shown, then click in the *Replace with:* box (also circled) and type *a*.

> *A dialogue box can have multiple **tickboxes** enabling various options. You can tick any combination of these depending on what you want to happen. Clicking again in a box that's ticked clears it.*

Word is now ready to search through our document, replacing *the* with *a* when it finds it. Because you ticked *Match case*, it won't change *The* at the start of each sentence. Put the mouse cursor over the *Find and Replace* dialogue box's titlebar and drag the box so that you can see the text in the document.

Click [Replace]. This moves to and highlights the next *the*.

> *Illogically, Word doesn't replace the text that was initially highlighted.*

Click [Replace] again. This changes *the* to *a* and highlights the next *the*. Suppose you don't want to change that one. Click [Find Next]. Word leaves it unchanged and highlights the one after.

> *You can click Edit > Find... if you just want to find a particular word or name in your document. If you click near the word in the document, you can make changes. The Find dialogue box remains open: you can click [Find Next] to find the next place that the word or name occurs.*

Let's be brave and click [Replace All]. That changes any remaining words *the* to *a*. When asked whether to continue searching at the beginning, click [Yes].

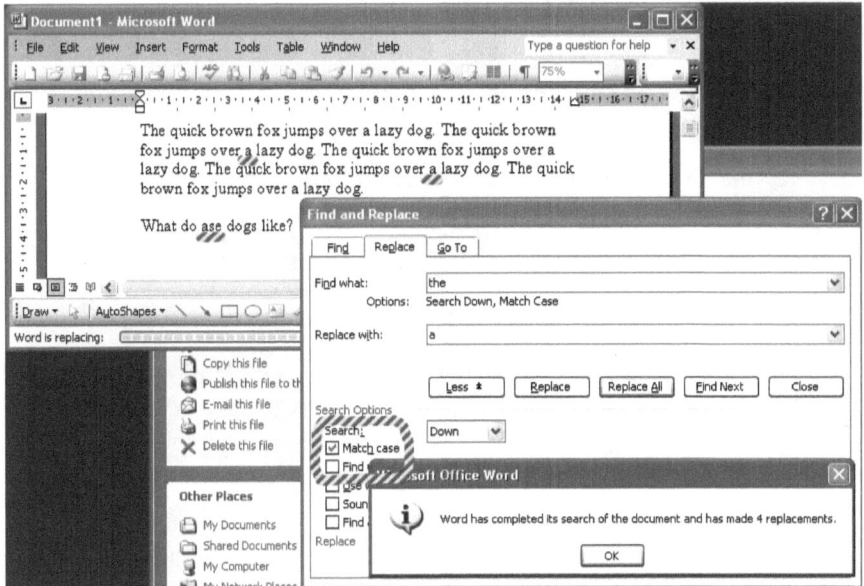

Uh-oh. Word changed *the* in places you wanted to leave unchanged and it also changed *the* in the word *these* so it now reads *ase*. You could have avoided the last unwanted change by also ticking *Find whole words only* but it's too late now.

Click on [OK], then on [Close] to close the *Find and Replace* box.

Click *Edit > Undo Replace All*. If you prefer, just press the shortcut key which is CTRL+Z.

Word remembers each change that you make to your document. **Undo** undoes them one by one. You've undone the changes you made when you clicked [Replace All]. Don't bother trying to redo them.

> There's a limit to how many changes you can undo but it's generous. If you accidentally undo more changes than you intended, you can **redo** them by clicking Edit > Redo. Unfortunately you can only redo changes in the same order you made them originally: there isn't a way to skip some of them.
>
> [Replace All] *is always a dangerous button to click. If you haven't carefully thought out all the possible places that something might match the Find what: text, unexpected things can get changed too. In a long document, you might not spot this until it was too late to undo the changes. All the same,*

Replace All *saves time if you need to make a lot of changes in the document and the Find what: text is unusual (e.g. a misspelled word where you've taken care to tick Find whole words only).*

Suppose you have a document describing the duties of two people: Alice and Bob. You decide their roles should be swapped. You can't just start by using **Replace All** *to change Alice to Bob everywhere. If you do that, Bob will have all the jobs and* **Replace All** *could only give them all to Alice.*

What you can do is to use **Replace All** *to change Alice to a nonsense sequence of characters that never occur elsewhere in your document, e.g. abcxyz. You can then use* **Replace All** *to change Bob to Alice and finally use it again to change abcxyz to Bob.*

Press CTRL+A. All the text in the document is selected and highlighted. Press SPACEBAR.

Oops. What happened?

The text you just selected (the whole document in this case) was replaced with a single space. Don't panic. *Edit > Undo* or CTRL+Z undoes that mistake too.

What you learned:

- **How to quickly select (highlight) a word.**
- **What a dialogue box is and how to move (drag) it.**
- **What tickboxes are and how to tick and clear them.**
- **That Word can search for a particular sequence of letters, e.g. a word, part of a word or a phrase (several words with spaces in between).**
- **That Word can quickly and easily replace that sequence with something different.**
- **That Word can do this everywhere in your document in an instant.**
- **That the computer does exactly what you tell it to do, even if that isn't what you wanted.**
- **You can undo recent changes to your document if something goes wrong.**

- This includes the heart-stopping case where your document disappears completely because you accidentally replaced it all with a single space.
- *You can redo changes if you accidentally undo too many of them.*
- *How to use* [Replace All] *to swap two words such as names.*

4.6 Selecting

You've seen a number of ways to select words in a document. Selecting is something you'll do often and it's useful to know how to do it quickly and easily.

- You can select text in a document by placing the mouse cursor at one end of it, then holding down the left mouse button and dragging to the other end of the selection.
- You can select everything in a document with *Edit > Select All* or by pressing CTRL+A.
- In Word, double-clicking selects a word while triple-clicking selects a whole paragraph. Other programs may be slightly different but you can always try different clicks (including quadruple-clicking) and see what happens.

After you've selected something, you can **extend** the selection by holding down SHIFT and clicking where you want the selection to start or end. For example, suppose you want to select several pages of a document. You can't see them all on the screen at the same time and selecting by dragging with the mouse is tricky. Instead, select the first word you want on the first page, then use the scroll bar to go to and see the last word you want in the selection. While holding down SHIFT, click just after it.

There are many things you can do with a selection. You can delete it using either the DELETE or BACKSPACE key. You can replace it with whatever is on the clipboard using *Edit > Paste* or CTRL+V. You can also replace selected text by typing something new.

You can put a selection on the clipboard with *Edit > Cut* (CTRL+X) or *Edit > Copy* (CTRL+C). **Cut** moves the selection to the clipboard. **Copy** leaves the selection in place and puts a new copy on the clipboard.

You can also click ✂ on the toolbar to cut the selection.

What you learned:

- Things can be selected by dragging over them or, in many cases, clicking on them.
- You can extend a selection by holding down SHIFT and clicking.
- You can select everything in the document using *Edit > Select All* or CTRL+A.
- You can delete a selection with DELETE or BACKSPACE.
- The difference between cutting and copying something to the clipboard.

There are many more things you can do with selections that you'll be seeing later on.

4.7 Paragraphs, margins, indents and tabs

Before you typed the last line of our document, you pressed the RETURN key twice. Pressing RETURN tells Word to start a new paragraph. Pressing it twice made Word put a paragraph consisting of a completely blank line between our two paragraphs. This makes it easy to see where the second paragraph starts.

Section 6.4 shows another way to add space between paragraphs.

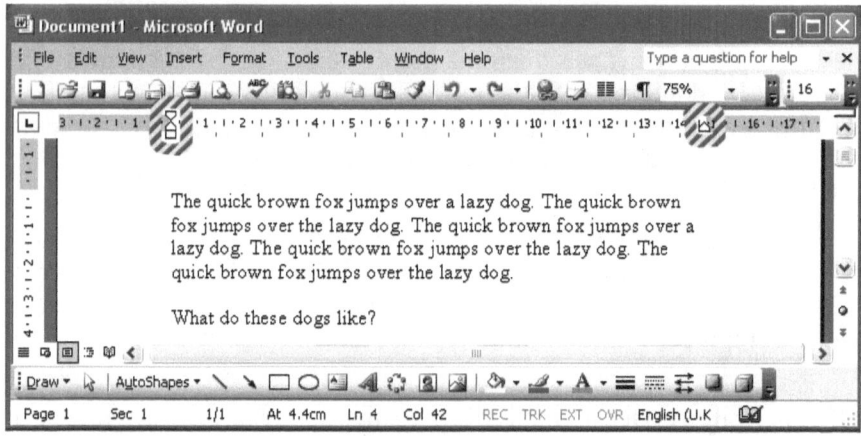

At each end of the ruler above the document, there are small sliders circled above. Place the text cursor anywhere in the first paragraph, then try dragging the sliders along the ruler.

> *If you don't see the ruler, click the View menu and click in the box to the left of Ruler so that a tick mark appears.*

The slider at the right hand end sets the right margin. As it's dragged to the left, lines of text in the first paragraph get shorter.

The top slider at the left sets the starting position for the first line in the paragraph. Dragging the bottom slider at the left sets the starting position for the remaining lines in the paragraph.

> *There's also a ruler at the left hand side. Numbers on the rulers show distances on the printed page (they may be different on the screen). Screenshots in this book have the rulers set to show distances in centimetres.*

> *You can change the units by clicking Tools > Options. A dialogue box appears. Click on the General tab, then choose Measurement units from the drop-down list. E.g. you can make the rulers show distances in inches.*

If you drag the bottom left slider away from the left-hand end of the ruler, you can position the top left slider to its left. This **outdents** the first line of the paragraph – something you might occasionally want to do.

The sliders are only affecting the first paragraph because that's where you put the text cursor. If you had selected all or part of a number of paragraphs (or all of them with CTRL+A), the sliders would affect all the selected paragraphs at the same time.

Drag all the sliders back to where they originally were, then drag the top left one to the right to **indent** the paragraph.

Click after the question mark after *like* to put the text cursor there. Press TAB and type *Walkies*. Press TAB again and type *Chasing things*. Press RETURN, then TAB, and type *Eating*. Press TAB again and type *Barking*. Press TAB again and type *Sleeping*.

> **Tab** *is an abbreviation of Tabulator. This is a key on a traditional typewriter that's used when typing a table.*

Drag with the mouse to select part or all of the last two lines. Click on the ruler above the start of the word *Walkies*. ⌐ appears on the ruler and *Walkies* and *Eating* both start below it. Click on the ruler again a bit to the right of *Walkies*. Another ⌐ appears and *Chasing things* and *Barking* both start below it. You've set two **tab stops**.

> *You can use tabs to arrange text in columns.*

4.7 Paragraphs, margins, indents and tabs

> There are default tab stops to the right of the two that you set. Sleeping is lined up with one of them.

Drag the ┗ marks along the ruler and the text below in both lines moves with them. The lines are separate paragraphs because you pressed RETURN between them but, as when setting indents, tab changes affect all selected paragraphs.

> To get rid of a tab stop, place the mouse pointer over its ┗, hold down the left mouse button and drag it down away from the ruler.

> When you outdent a paragraph, the bottom left slider also acts as a tab stop. For example, if you're typing a glossary, you can set up outdenting and press TAB after each word that you define. The first word after the TAB will line up with the start of subsequent lines.

> If you double-click any of the tab stops on the ruler, a dialogue box opens where you see a list of all the tab stops you've set. You can choose one of them by its position and change its type. With the usual Left stop, the first character following the tab will be aligned with the stop. The other stop types work on all the text you type following the tab up to another tab or the end of the line. A Right stop aligns the end of the text with the stop and a Centred stop centres it on the stop. A Decimal stop is similar to a Right stop but, if the text contains a decimal point, it's aligned with the stop. This is used to set up a column of numbers, e.g. prices.

> A Bar stop doesn't affect the alignment of the text but it causes a vertical line to appear at its position which you can use to separate columns of text.

What you learned:

- **Pressing RETURN starts a new paragraph.**
- **How to change the left and right margins.**
- **How to indent or outdent paragraphs.**
- **How to set and adjust tabs to create columns of text.**
- **That, if you don't set tab stops, default tab positions are used.**
- **That margins, indents and outdents and tabs can apply to one, several or all paragraphs in a document.**

- *How to make the rulers appear.*
- *How to change the dimension units on the ruler.*
- *How to remove a tab stop.*
- *An easy way to format a glossary.*
- *The difference between a Left, Right, Centred and Decimal tab stop.*

4.8 Word Wrapping and Justification

You'll have noticed, when you adjusted the right margin of the first paragraph of the document, that Word automatically chose the word beginning each line of the paragraph so that the previous line fitted nicely. This is automatic **word-wrapping**.

The lines in a paragraph are also automatically adjusted when you add or delete text or if you change the text font, which you'll be doing soon.

You can see why you should only press RETURN when you want to start a new paragraph. Not only don't you need to press RETURN at the end of a line within a paragraph, doing it causes problems. Word treats the next line as a new paragraph and the word-wrapping won't work correctly if you make changes later.

> *There are times when you want to start a new line without it starting a new paragraph. Holding down SHIFT and pressing RETURN does this: it's called a* **line break**.
>
> *Holding down CTRL and pressing RETURN starts a new paragraph on a new page. This is known as a* **page break**.

When Word decides to start a new line in a paragraph, it's unlikely that the previous line will be exactly the right length to extend to the right-hand margin. Usually, it'll be a bit shorter. There are four ways to deal with the leftover space.

The simplest answer is to leave it all at the right hand end of the line. All lines start at the left hand margin but most end a bit before the right-hand one. This is known as **left-justified**: it's what you've used so far.

Things can be reversed so that the leftover space is on the left hand side and all lines end at the right margin. This is **right-justified** text – it isn't used often.

Another option is to split the leftover space equally between the two ends of each line so that the line is **centred** between the margins.

The last option is to add the leftover space equally between words on the line and sometimes also between letters in each word. This allows each line to start at the left margin and end exactly at the right margin too. It's known as **fully-justified** text. Newspapers, magazines and books often use full justification but it can look too formal in other documents.

You've probably spotted that each of these four paragraphs uses the justification that it describes: left, right, centred and full.

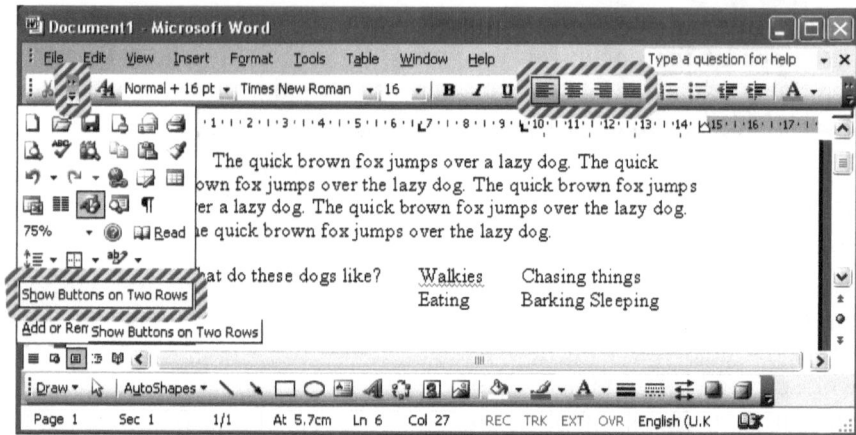

To set the justification for one or more paragraphs, place the cursor there or select the paragraphs, then click one of the four buttons circled in the picture above.

Word automatically hides buttons that you haven't used recently: you might not be able to see the four buttons. If so, click on any (one of them is circled above), then click on *Show Buttons on Two Rows*.

What you learned:

- **How word-wrapping works.**
- **Why you should only press RETURN to start a new paragraph.**
- **What text justification is and how to set it. This includes centring text.**
- **How to see more buttons on the toolbar.**
- *How to start a new line within a paragraph by pressing SHIFT+RETURN.*

- *How to start a new page by pressing CTRL+RETURN.*

4.9 Styles, Typefaces and Fonts

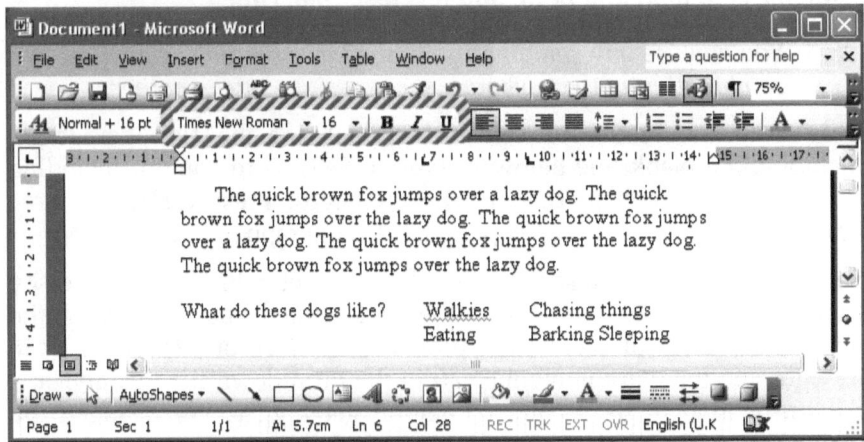

Two drop-down **selector boxes** are circled along with three **style** buttons to their right.

> Move the mouse cursor over **B** (one of the style buttons) without clicking it. A small box appears saying Bold. Move it over **I** and a box appears saying Italic. Move it over **U** and a box appears saying Underline. These are **tooltips**: they tell you what the button does.
>
> Many on-screen buttons in various programs have tooltips.

Drag over the first and second sentences of the first paragraph to select them, then click **B** or press the equivalent keyboard shortcut: CTRL+B. The words become darker and more prominent – **the style is now Bold**.

Click the mouse anywhere in the document to unselect the two sentences, then select the first sentence on its own. **B** is still highlighted, showing that the words are in bold. Click the button. It's no longer highlighted and the first sentence is back to normal. The second sentence is still in bold.

> Each time you click one of the three style buttons, the style is either applied to or removed from the selected text.

Select the third sentence and click **I** or press CTRL+I. The words are slanting – *the style is Italic.*

Select the fourth sentence and click **U** or press CTRL+U. <u>The sentence is underlined</u>.

Select the fifth sentence and click all three buttons in succession. ***<u>The sentence is in bold and italic and it is also underlined</u>***.

> *You can use any combination of the three buttons or any combination of the keyboard shortcuts one after another.*

Drag with the mouse to select the whole of the first paragraph, including the blank line below it. Press CTRL+C to copy it, including its end-of-paragraph marker, to the clipboard. Press CTRL+V three times so that there are three copies of the paragraph.

Select the whole of the second copy by dragging with the mouse or by triple-clicking in it, then go to the box circled above showing the number *16* (on your screen, it'll probably show 10 or 12). Click ▼ to its right and then on the number *20* in the drop-down list that appears. All the words in the second paragraph get bigger. We changed the paragraph to 20 point.

> *The size of printed characters is traditionally given in **points**, measured from the top of a tall character such as h to the bottom of a descender, e.g. in j. A point is 1/72 of an inch (0.353 mm). 10 point is the smallest size you should normally use – anything smaller could be classed as "fine print" although newspapers often use smaller print and are still quite legible. 12 point is easier to read and you'll want to use larger sizes again for headings, etc.*
>
> *Word normally defaults to 10 or 12 point text. Screenshots prepared for this book use 16 point text to make it easier to see.*

Select the third paragraph, then go to the box circled above showing *Times New Roman*. Click ▼ to its right. A list of **typefaces** installed on your computer appears. There may be too many to show them all. If so, there will be a scrollbar next to the list. Scroll up, find *Arial* and click on it.

The typeface of the third paragraph changes from Times New Roman to Arial. Times New Roman is a so-called **serif** typeface – the letters have small lines across their ends.

Arial is a simpler **sans-serif** typeface.

Arial and Times New Roman are proportional fonts – each letter is just as wide as it needs to be. The widest letter is m, others such as i are narrower.

Another typeface worth mentioning is Courier. This is a **monospaced** font – all letters are spaced far enough apart for an m to fit.

`Courier looks as if it was typed on a typewriter.`

In traditional printing, a **font** is a box of cast metal letters of a particular typeface, point size and style (e.g. italic) but people often say font when they mean typeface. For example, they might say to use Times New Roman as the font for a document that contains text of various styles and point sizes.

Windows uses its installed fonts to convert the letter codes stored by programs running on the computer into the shape of the corresponding letter on the screen or on paper in the printer. For example, the letter A is stored in memory as a single byte (8 bits) but this code is converted to a pattern of several hundred or thousand dots to make the shape of an A on the screen or on paper with a particular typeface, point size and style.

Sometimes Windows has different versions of a font installed to produce the different styles. If not, it modifies the normal style of the font (e.g. by widening the lines or slanting the characters).

Arial, Courier and Times New Roman are usually present on any Windows computer. Depending which other fonts are installed, you may have many other typefaces in the list - some of them very fancy.

You'll have problems if a document is moved to a different computer that doesn't have a font that you used installed on it. This often happens if you e-mail the document to someone else. Their computer will automatically choose a similar font that it does have installed but the match may not be good.

You can highlight individual words or even letters within a word and change their typeface, size and style.

As a rule of thumb, you should avoid using more than two or three different typefaces in the same document. Using too many looks messy.

Drag to select the first sentence of the third paragraph. Click *Format > Change Case...*. A dialogue box opens.

The circles are known as **Radio buttons**. *Like the station buttons on a car radio and unlike tickboxes (Section 4.5), only one can be selected at a time – the previous choice is automatically cleared.*

Click on the circle next to UPPERCASE to select it as shown above, then click [OK]. The sentence changes to all capitals.

Other choices are Sentence case where only the first letter of a sentence is capitalised, all lower case and Title Case where the first letter of each word is capitalised. tOGGLE cASE is useful if you typed something without noticing that CAPS LOCK was on.

You could have pressed RETURN instead of clicking [OK]. When a button is highlighted, you can press RETURN instead of clicking it.

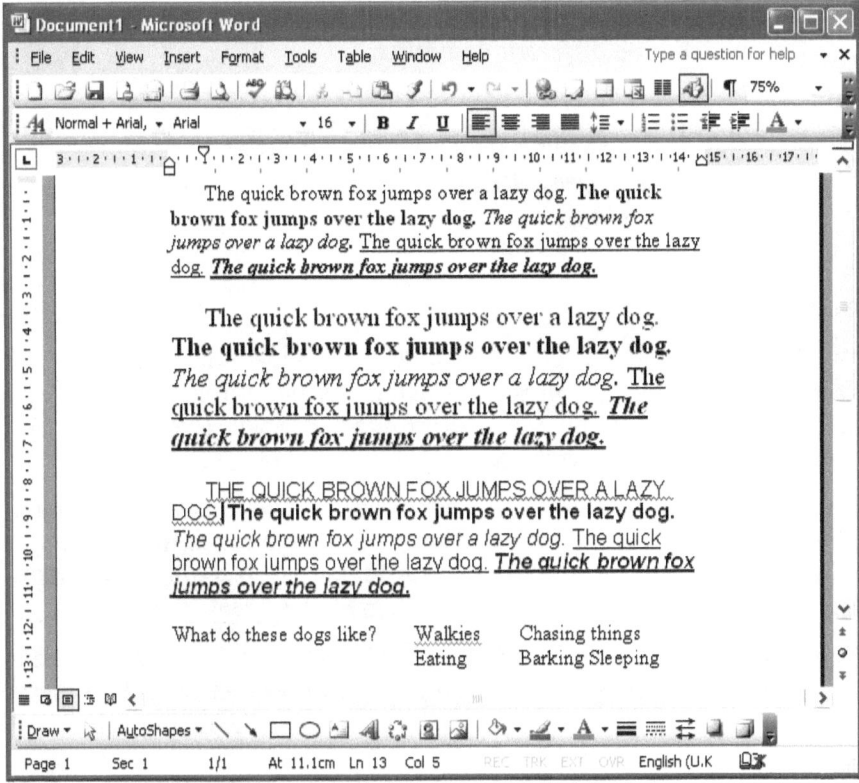

What you learned:

- What text styles are and how to set and unset them.
- That text styles can be used in any combination.
- What a typeface is.
- How to change the size and typeface of text.
- The difference between serif and sans-serif typefaces.
- How to change the capitalisation of text.
- *What tooltips are.*
- *The difference between proportional and mono-spaced typefaces.*
- *That text size is measured in points.*
- *What a font is (it can mean two different things) and how the computer uses it.*

4.9 Styles, Typefaces and Fonts

- *That you can have problems with fonts when a document is opened on a different computer.*
- *Not to go overboard with too many different typefaces.*
- *What Radio buttons are and how they differ from tickboxes.*
- *That you can press RETURN instead of clicking on a highlighted button.*

4.10 Symbols

Windows has fonts such as Webdings and Wingdings which contain symbols like ♛ or ⊕ instead of letters. Ordinary fonts such as Arial and Times New Roman include foreign alphabets (e.g. Greek) and some commonly-used symbols such as ©.

To insert a symbol at the text cursor position, click *Insert > Symbol....* The *Symbol* dialogue box opens. Choose a font and look for the symbol you want. You may need to try several fonts (e.g. *Webdings*) and scroll down to find it. Click on the symbol, then click [Insert].

The dialogue box stays open. You can drag it so you can see your document, click somewhere else in it and insert another symbol there. Once you've finished, click [Close] to close the dialogue box.

> *You can copy and paste a symbol already in your document anywhere else that you need it. Double-clicking on a symbol opens the Symbol dialogue box: you can see which font it's in. If you need a related symbol it'll probably be available in that font too.*
>
> *Symbols are stored in memory just like letters: it's the font selection that makes them look different. If you accidentally change the typeface for some of your text to a symbol font such as Wingdings, it'll start showing as meaningless symbols. Don't panic, just change it back.*

What you learned:

- **That Windows has special fonts which contain symbols instead of letters.**
- **That ordinary fonts can include foreign alphabets and some symbols.**
- **How to find and insert the symbols you want into your document.**

- *How to find related symbols that may be available in the same font.*
- *That you can copy and paste symbols.*
- *What happens if you accidentally select a symbol font.*

4.11 Non-printing characters

You'll remember that the teleprinter machine in Chapter 2 punched a special pattern of holes in the tape when the spacebar was pressed and that this moved the print position on by one place without printing anything when the words on the tape were printed. Other special patterns would be punched if the TAB or RETURN keys were pressed. Your computer stores these same patterns as special characters (bytes) in its memory when you press those keys.

> *Two different special characters can be stored when the RETURN key is pressed. Carriage Return (CR) tells a teleprinter to move its printing position to the start of the line and Line Feed (LF) tells it to advance the paper to a new line. Windows stores the CR-LF sequence when RETURN is pressed while Unix-based systems including Linux and Apple's OS-X store LF only. Older Apple systems store CR only. This can cause problems when files produced by some programs are transferred between different types of computer. Fortunately, files created by Word don't suffer from this problem.*

Click *Tools > Options*. A dialogue box opens (shown later on). Click the *View tab* and click the *All* box under *Formatting marks* so it's ticked. Click [OK]. You'll see apparent changes in your document. There's a small dot between most of the words. You'll see → between words where you pressed TAB and you'll see a paragraph marker (¶) wherever you pressed RETURN.

> *A common minor mistake is to unintentionally put more than one space between words when typing. With non-printing characters visible, you can spot extra dots where they shouldn't be and delete them.*
>
> *You can also use Edit > Replace... to get rid of unwanted spaces, whether they're visible or not. Put the cursor in the Find what: box and press the spacebar twice. Put the cursor in the Replace with: box and press the spacebar once. You can now*

> *track down any unintentional sequences of two (or more) spaces and get rid of one of them by clicking* [Replace].

Select the word *Barking* by double-clicking it. Place the mouse cursor over it and press and hold down the left mouse or trackpad button. While still holding the button down, move the cursor between → and *Eating*. Release the button.

You see *Barking Eating*. You moved the highlighted word by dragging and dropping but it's not right. Press CTRL+Z to undo it.

> *Intellisense added the space between Barking and Eating.*

Place the mouse cursor just before *Barking* and drag to just before *Sleeping*. *Barking* is now highlighted along with the → after it: the word is selected along with the special TAB character. Retry dragging and dropping it to just before *Eating*. This time, it works properly: *Barking* and *Eating* are lined up with the tab marks on the ruler.

> *You can also copy selected text by dragging and dropping. Hold down the CTRL key while dragging. The original selected text remains and a copy is dropped at the cursor position.*

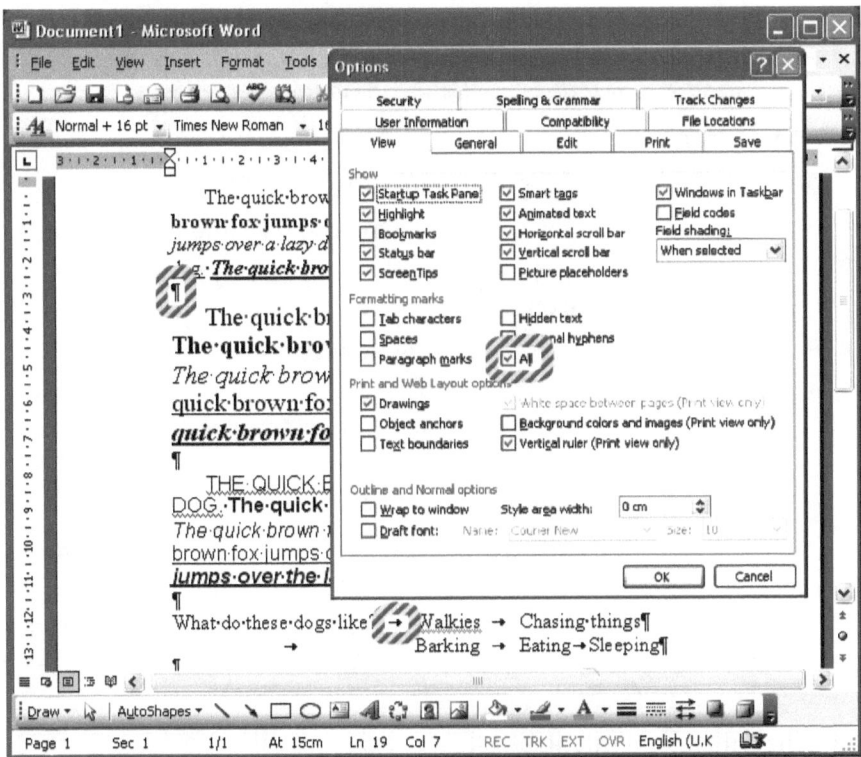

Instead of using *Tools > Options*, you can turn the special markers on and off by pressing CTRL+*. Try pressing this several times (you'll usually need to hold down SHIFT too). The markers appear and disappear. Leave them off.

> The markers for non-printing characters won't appear when you print your document, even when they're visible on the screen.

> Dragging and dropping and other editing such as replacing highlighted text or cutting and copying it to the clipboard works just the same when the special markers are not visible. If you want to include a space, tab or paragraph marker, you need to highlight the blank space on the screen where the marker would be.

> Other non-printing characters are used to record changes in the text formatting such as different indents, justification, typefaces and text styles and sizes. Although they can't be made visible, they're also moved by cutting or copying and pasting or by dragging and dropping. The results of this aren't always what

4.11 Non-printing characters   47 *you'd expect or want. In particular, you should keep an eye on the text that was before and after something that you move to make sure that it doesn't change in an unexpected way.*

What you learned:

- **What non-printing characters are.**
- **How to make non-printing characters visible on the screen.**
- **How to move or copy selected (highlighted) text by dragging and dropping.**
- *That you may need to include non printing characters when you move text around.*
- *That text formatting also uses non printing characters that you can't make visible.*
- *That these can cause problems when you move text.*
- *That different computers use incompatible ways of recording when RETURN is pressed.*
- *How to find and remove unintentional extra spaces between words.*

4.12 Checking your spelling

Try deliberately misspelling a word in the document, then move the text cursor elsewhere. Word looks to see if the word is in its dictionary. When it can't find it, it puts a wavy red line under it. Move the mouse cursor over the offending word and right-click.

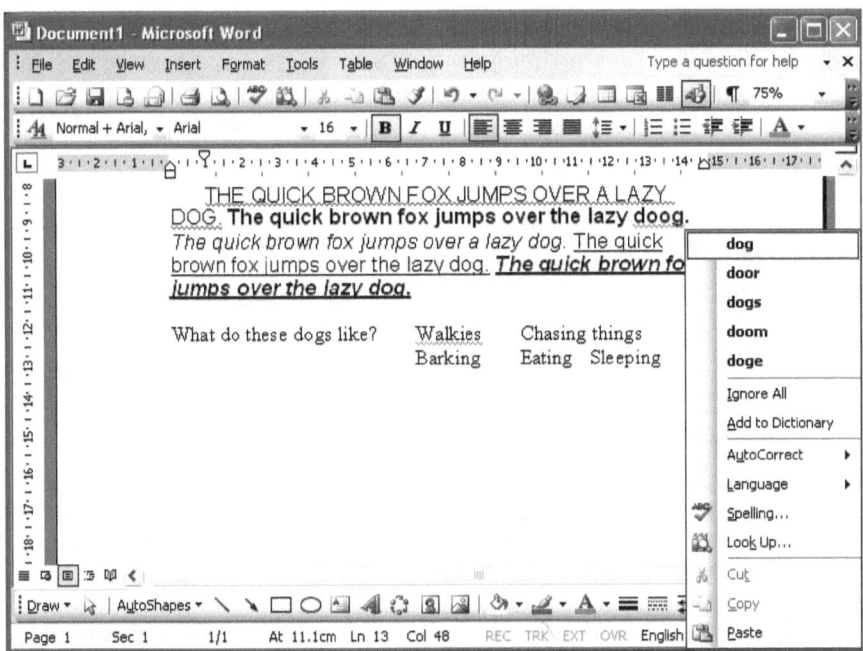

You see a list of possible replacements for the word. Click on the correct one. The word is replaced.

You'll notice that *Walkies* has a wavy red line. This is because it isn't in the dictionary but it doesn't mean that you must change the word. The wavy line won't appear when you print the document. If you want to, right-click the word and choose *Ignore All* to ignore all instances of the word in the document. You can use *Add to Dictionary* to add the word to the dictionary so that it will be accepted in all your documents.

> You can have multiple spell-check dictionaries installed, e.g. for different languages.
>
> Spell checkers can't spot cases where you've used a wrong sound-alike word that's also in the dictionary. E.g. "I ran this threw the spell chequer sew I know its write".

You'll also notice that the sentence you changed to UPPERCASE has a wavy green line under it. Word has a grammar checker and it thinks something might be wrong with the sentence. It spots many other errors such as a sentence without a verb but it can be excessively picky.

If you click *Tools > Spelling and Grammar...*, Word checks the whole document for misspelled words and possible grammatical errors. When it finds one, it shows a dialogue box where you can make the same choices as above. This saves you from having to go through the whole document looking for wavy lines.

What you learned:

- **What the wavy red and green lines mean and what to do about them.**
- **How to spell and grammar check the whole document.**
- *What a spell-checker can't do.*

4.13 Saving the document

Click *File > Save As...*, press CTRL+S or click on ![] (circled below).

Even though floppy disks are rarely used any more, the ![] icon lives on.

The *Save As* dialogue box appears. You haven't given the document a name yet so Word has chosen one based on the start of the document. It's highlighted but it's not very convenient. You can just type a suitable name, e.g. *LazyDog*. Click Save.

The document is copied from your computer's RAM to its hard disk. Now it's safely stored as a file even if the computer crashes, is turned off or decides to restart after an update.

Word saves documents in the My Documents folder but you can choose a different folder if you want. Folders are explained in Chapter 5.

*Word normally automatically saves any changes you've made to a special file every 10 minutes or so. If it or the computer crashes or there's a power failure, you'll be offered the chance to **recover** your document when you start Word again. Some of your most recent changes may still be lost.*

Now that the document has a name, it shows this instead of *Document1* on its titlebar. If you make more changes and save it again (by clicking 💾 or *File > Save* or pressing CTRL+S), the changed version immediately replaces the one on the hard disk without you being asked for its name. If you want to keep the old version and save the new version in a different folder and/or with a different name, you can click *File > Save As...* to open the dialogue box.

What you learned:

- **How to give your document a name and save it to the hard disk.**
- **How to save the document again after you've made changes to it.**
- **How to save a new version of the document with a different name.**
- *That you can recover most of your document after a crash.*

4.14 Printing the document

Things can sometimes go wrong when you try to print a document. You already saved it – it won't be lost even if the computer locks up or crashes.

Click *File > Print....* A dialogue box opens

You might have more than one printer set up on your computer. Make sure that the right one is shown: if it isn't, click on ▼, then on the name of the printer you want to use in the list that appears. Make sure that the printer is switched on and isn't out of paper.

> *If you don't see the printer you want, it may not be installed (set up) on your computer. You'll need to look at the instructions that came with the printer to see how to do this.*

You want to print the whole of your document. Make sure that the radio button to the left of *All* under *Page range* (one of the three circled above) is filled in.

> *If you have a long document and don't want to print all of it, click on the radio button to the left of Pages: under Page range. Type the page numbers you want to print in the box to the right of Pages:.*

> *The page numbers should be typed with commas between them. You can also specify ranges of pages by putting dashes between them. E.g. 1,3,5-7,10- will print pages 1, 3, 5, 6, 7 and page 10 onwards.*

*You'll notice that the dialogue box lets you print several copies at once and choose whether to have them collated. If you choose not to **collate**, the printer prints all copies of each page together. They will print faster (especially if the pages include graphics) but you'll need to put them in order by hand afterwards.*

Click [OK]. The document is printed – perhaps after a short delay.

One of your printers will be set as the default. If you want to print the whole document to it, you can click 🖨 on the toolbar instead of using File > Print.... When you move the mouse cursor over the 🖨 button, the tool-tip shows which printer would be used.

Click ☒ to close Word.

If you forget to save the file or if you've made changes since it was last saved, you'll be asked whether you want to save or discard your changes.

What you learned:

- **How to print a document.**
- **How to select the printer you want to use and the pages you want to print.**
- *That it's wise to save your document before you try to print it.*
- *How to choose which pages and how many copies to print.*
- *What collation is and when you might not want to use it.*
- *How to print the whole document with a single click.*
- *That Word will try to make sure that you save your document before closing the program.*

4.15 Documents attached to an e-mail

You can send a file to someone else by **attaching** it to an e-mail. This book doesn't attempt to describe how to send and receive e-mails. There are too many different e-mail programs and systems.

However, there's a very important thing you need to know.

Windows has special temporary folders on the hard disk where it keeps files that are only needed for a short time. When you click on a document on a web page or attached to an e-mail, a copy is put in one of these folders and your word processor is started and told to open it.

Sometimes, the word processor knows that the document is in a temporary folder and prevents you from making any changes until you've saved it in a safe permanent location.

> *If you're swearing at your computer because it won't let you edit a document, this could be the reason.*

But all too often the word processor lets you work all day on the document, then click ▣. What you don't realise is that the version with all your changes was written back to the temporary folder. Windows may decide at any time that it's not needed any more and delete it. Even if the file isn't deleted, it's often impossible to find out where it's hidden.

> *Many people I know have lost hours of work because of this.*

Always use *File > Save as...* and choose a folder such as *My Documents* before you start work on any document that you opened directly from an e-mail or web page.

5 Files and folders

This chapter explains how documents, etc. are stored on your computer's hard disk and how to access, organise and move them.

5.1 The hard disk

Click **start**, then on *My Computer*. A window appears.

There are icons looking like folders in a filing cabinet and various kinds of disk drives.

Click on the circled hard disk drive labelled *(C:)* - it may have another name too but this varies. If clicking highlights the drive but doesn't open it, try double clicking it. You should now see a number of icons looking like the **folders** you'd find in a filing cabinet.

> You need to be able to select disk drives, folders and files or open them. Windows can be set to use either of two methods:
>
> - With the first method, clicking selects a disk drive, folder or file and double-clicking opens it.
>
> - With the second method, pausing the mouse cursor over the disk drive, folder or file selects it. This is called **hover select**. A single click opens it.
>
> Now you know how to open a disk drive, folder or file by clicking on it, we will merely say Open.

What you're looking at is the **root folder** of your hard disk. It contains a *WINDOWS* folder which holds the Windows operating system programs. There's also a *Program Files* folder containing programs you've added. Don't mess with either of these folders unless you really know what you're doing.

> Each folder has a name and it can contain files. A file is like a length of paper tape punched with the bytes that make up the document or program. Imagine that a name is written on it and it's stored in a folder in a filing cabinet.
>
> A folder can contain other folders – this would be useful in a real filing cabinet too but it would be physically hard to achieve.
>
> You can't have two files or folders with the same name in the same folder because the computer would be as confused as you'd be.
>
> A folder may also be called a **directory**: they're the same thing.

Open *Documents and Settings*. You should see a number of folders. One of these has your Windows account name. Open it.

> Unfortunately, your account and user name may not be the same. You might have to try a couple of different folders.

You now see icons or a list of your personal files and folders. If there are many of them, there will be a scroll bar to the right. Use it to move down until you see folders called *Desktop* and *My Documents*.

> Windows Vista is slightly different from XP. The folder for your Windows account is in Users rather than Documents and Settings and the folder containing your documents is called Documents rather than My Documents. There may still be a My Documents folder but it's likely to be empty. When we refer to the My Documents folder, we mean Documents if you're using Vista.

Open *My Documents* and click *View > Details* to see a detailed list of files and folders in it. Mentally note some of their names. Your Word document *LazyDog* should be there although you might not spot it immediately.

> When you save a new file, Word saves it in My Documents unless you choose a different folder.

Click or double-click on *LazyDog*. It opens: Word starts and displays it. You aren't going to do anything with it. Click ☒ to close it and click ☒ again to close the *My Documents* folder.

What you learned:

- **What folders and files are.**
- **That they have icons and names.**
- **How to open a folder or a file such as a document.**
- **That you have a personal folder in *Documents and Settings* with a *Desktop* and a *My Documents* folder in it.**
- **That Word saved the *LazyDog* document in your *My Documents* folder.**
- **That you can start with the root of the hard disk and work your way to any file on the disk but it's tedious**
- *That programs are kept as files in folders that you should leave alone.*
- *That a folder and a directory are the same thing.*
- *That the names for some folders are different in Vista.*

5.2 Finding files and making folders

Click ⊞ start , then move the mouse pointer over *My Documents* at the top right of the box that appears and click. This takes you directly to the folder containing the word processor file – it contains the same files and folders that you just noted. It's a much easier and faster way to get there.

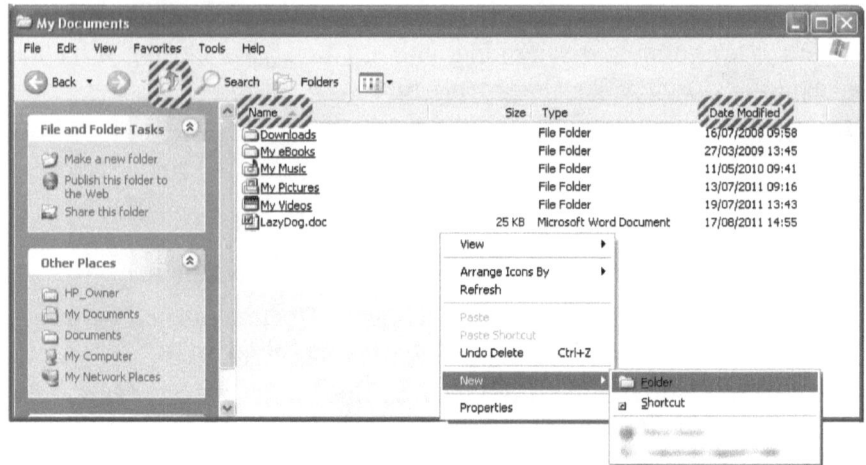

Click *View > Details*. The files and folders are shown in a list with *Size* and *Date Modified* as shown above.

If you click on *Name* (circled), the files and folders are sorted alphabetically. The triangle next to *Name* shows that this is the order. Click on *Name* again. The triangle flips over and the sorting order is reversed.

Click on *Date Modified* (circled). The triangle appears next to this and the files and folders are sorted by the date and time that the last change to them was made. This is very useful if you can't remember the name of a file that you need to find but you know approximately when it was created or changed.

> *You can sort on any of the other columns instead. Just click on the column title.*

Right-click in the window to the right of the file names. A small box appears as shown above. Move the cursor over *New* in the box. Another small box appears. Click on *Folder* in this box. A folder appears with the name *New Folder* highlighted. Type *WP files* and press RETURN.

You just made a brand new folder. Its name was set to *New Folder* but, because it was highlighted, anything you typed replaced the name and it's now called *WP files*. Open it. Of course it's empty - you only just made it.

Click on (circled above). That takes you to the folder that contains the one you're currently viewing. You're back in the *My Documents* folder.

Chapter 5 Files and folders

The Type column in the list shows whether a file is a program or some kind of data file such as a word processor document or a spreadsheet, picture, sound, etc. Windows knows which type it is because its file name has a dot at the end followed by an **extension**, *often three letters. Examples of extensions are .exe for a program, .doc for a Word document, .jpg for a picture or .mp3 for a music file. Depending on option settings, you may not see the file name extensions.*

If you open a file whose extension is .exe, Windows knows to copy it into RAM and start running it as a program. Other types of file are **associated** *with programs already installed on the computer. When you click on one of those, Windows starts the program and tells it to open the file you clicked on.*

Vista doesn't have the 📁 button. The folder you're currently in and the folders containing it are listed in a box at the top. You can go to any of them by clicking the name in the box.

What you learned:

- **My Documents is a special folder – you can get to it quickly via the Start button.**
- **You can list the contents of a folder in various orders including by name or by date modified – this helps when you're looking for a file.**
- **A way to create and name a new folder.**
- **You can use 📁 to get to the folder containing the one you were looking at.**
- *That Vista uses a different way to get to containing folders.*
- **What a file name extension is.**
- **How Windows uses extensions to know the type of a file and what program to use to open it.**

5.3 Using a thumbdrive

If you have a USB thumbdrive / Data Stick, plug it into any USB port on your computer. If in doubt, look at the rectangular metal connector on the thumbdrive, then look for a socket on the front or side of your computer that's the same size and shape.

USB (Universal Serial Bus) is a way to connect various devices to the computer including thumbdrives, external hard disks, printers and scanners. Music players, cameras and mobile phones can be connected with USB so you can copy files to and from them.

After a short delay, a window may appear showing the folders and files saved on the thumbdrive (there may not be any). Minimise it. It should appear as *Removable disk* on the taskbar.

Click **start**, then *My Computer*. As before, you see disk *(C:)* but you also see *Removable Disk* lower down. Open it. You'll see folders and files on the thumbdrive (if there are any) – the computer views it as another disk drive.

The thumbdrive may have a name which appears instead of Removable Disk.

You may now have Removable Disk twice on the taskbar. If so, you can close one of them.

Click on *My Documents* on the taskbar or, if it isn't there, open it from **start**. Select *LazyDog* by moving the cursor over it or by single-clicking it. Press CTRL+C to copy *LazyDog* to the clipboard. Click on *Removable disk* on the taskbar and press CTRL+V. *LazyDog* appears there.

Instead of copying and pasting, you could drag LazyDog onto the Removable Disk button on the taskbar, then onto the Removable Disk window, then release the button to drop it there. Windows leaves a copy in My Documents because you dragged it from there (on the hard disk) to a different disk.

Open *LazyDog* on *Removable Disk*. Word starts and displays your document. You aren't going to do anything with it and you can close it.

If you wanted, you could make changes to the document but, when they're saved, this will be on the thumbdrive and the copy on the hard disk remains as it was. This soon gets confusing. There's a risk of ending up with two different copies of the document where some changes are in one and some are in the other.

Near the right end of the taskbar, there are a number of small icons. If you move the cursor over it, *Safely Remove Hardware* appears. Click on the icon and then click on *Safely remove USB Mass Storage Device*.

Chapter 5 Files and folders

Once a message saying *Safe To Remove Hardware* appears, you can unplug the thumbdrive.

> *Saving changes on the thumbdrive can take some time. If you unplug it before "Safely remove USB Mass Storage Device" appears, there's a risk of losing files on it.*

> *If you don't see* 💾*, click* 🔘 *near the right end of the taskbar. More icons appear.* 💾 *should be one of them.*

If you plug the thumbdrive into a different computer, you can copy files from the thumbdrive to its hard drive. You may not be able to open the files unless the computer has the same programs installed on it. Again of course you must be sure that any changes you make are to the newest version of the document.

> *You can copy a document file such as LazyDog to a thumbdrive or removable disk and give it to someone or you can attach it to an e-mail and send it to them.*

Click on *My Documents* on the taskbar. Notice that *LazyDog* is still there.

What you learned:

- **How to plug in and safely unplug the thumbdrive**
- **That the computer sees it as another disk drive, even though there's no spinning disk.**
- **How to use the clipboard to copy a file such as a word processing document from the hard drive to the thumbdrive.**
- **How to use the thumbdrive to copy a file onto another computer.**
- *How to drag and drop a file or folder to a different drive.*
- *That, if you do this, Windows makes a new copy and leaves the original file or folder in place.*
- *That you can open and edit a document directly from the thumbdrive but this may not be a good idea.*

5.4 Moving files and creating shortcuts

Position the cursor over *LazyDog* in *My Documents*, then hold down the left mouse button. Move the mouse over the new *WP files* folder in the same window, then release the button. *LazyDog* is gone from the *My Documents* folder. It was dragged to the *WP files* folder.

Place the cursor over the *WP files* folder and right-click it. In the box that appears, click *Create Shortcut*. *Shortcut to WP files* appears.

Right-click on the new shortcut and, in the box that appears, click on *Cut*. Close the *My Documents* window and minimise any other windows that are obscuring the desktop. Right-click on a blank part of the desktop and, in the box that appears, click on *Paste*. *Shortcut to WP files* appears on the desktop.

> *You can cut, copy or paste a file or folder using the Edit menu or keyboard shortcut or by right-clicking.*
>
> *Files, folders and shortcuts can all be moved by cutting and pasting or by dragging and dropping. You can use whichever method is more convenient.*
>
> *You can select multiple files and/or folders using CTRL+A, by dragging the mouse cursor over them, by selecting them individually while holding down CTRL or by selecting the first one, then holding down SHIFT and selecting the last one in a list. Once you've selected them, you can copy or move them all at once. Pressing DELETE would delete them.*

Right-click *Shortcut to WP files* and, in the box that appears, click on *Rename*. The name *Shortcut to WP files* is highlighted. Type *WP files* and press RETURN. The name is changed.

Open *WP files* on the desktop by clicking or double-clicking. The *WP files* window reopens, containing *LazyDog*. You can now get there directly from your desktop.

> *A **shortcut file** is a pointer to another file or folder. Its icon includes a little arrow. You can put a shortcut in any folder, not just on the desktop. When you click to open a shortcut, Windows finds the file or folder that it points to and opens that instead.*

Right-click on *LazyDog*, move the cursor over *Send To* and click *Desktop (create shortcut)* in the box that appears.

> *This is a quicker way to put a shortcut to a file or folder on the desktop. You can rename the new shortcut (if you want) by right-clicking it on the Desktop and clicking on Rename.*

Click in the *WP files* window. You're now in *My Documents*. Click

🏃 again. This takes you to the *Desktop* folder. Notice that the two shortcuts you just placed on the desktop (*WP files* and *Shortcut to LazyDog*) are in this folder. *Desktop* is a special folder – anything it in appears on the computer desktop.

> As well as shortcuts, you can put documents and folders themselves on the Desktop. Section 5.5 explains why this often isn't a good idea.
>
> As you saw in Section 5.1, Desktop and My Documents are really both in a folder belonging to you as the computer user. If you'd opened My Documents that way, clicking 🏃 twice would have taken you there. Because you opened My Documents from `start` instead, Windows XP tries to be helpful and pretends My Documents is in Desktop. Helpful pah!!! It's just confusing.

Right-click on *My Documents* in the *Desktop* folder and click *Properties*. A dialogue box opens. Click on the *General* tab. The total size of all the files and folders in *My Documents* is shown. This will be useful information when you make a backup copy. Click `Cancel` or `X` to close the dialogue box.

> The dialogue box shows both Size and Size on disk. When a file is saved on a disk or thumbdrive, space is allocated in fixed chunks, e.g. 4096 bytes. Some of the space in the last chunk ends up unused so it takes up a bit of additional space on the disk.

Open *Shortcut to LazyDog* by clicking or double-clicking it on the desktop. Word starts and displays the document. Click `X` to close it.

> When a document has a shortcut on the desktop, it's very easy to open it.
>
> You can get rid of a shortcut by right-clicking it and choosing Delete: the file or folder that it points to isn't affected. But be sure it's a shortcut (with the little arrow): the file or folder itself might be on the desktop.
>
> When you delete a file, folder or shortcut, Windows moves it to the special **Recycle Bin** folder that you'll see on your desktop. If you deleted the file or folder accidentally, you can open the Recycle Bin, find it, right-click it and click Restore.
>
> You'll want to make folders in My Documents and organise your documents in them. It's up to you how to set up the folders: it's

like planning a filing cabinet although a bit more flexible. You can get to any of the folders from My Documents so you'll only want to put shortcuts on the desktop for the files and folders that you use most often. If you put too many shortcuts there, it gets messy and confusing.

What you learned:

- **How to move a file to a different folder on the same hard disk by dragging and dropping or by cutting and pasting.**
- **How to create a shortcut to a file or folder.**
- **How to get quickly to a folder or open a document by putting a shortcut on the desktop.**
- **That the desktop displays files, folders and shortcuts placed in the special Desktop folder.**
- **How to see the total size of all the files in a folder.**
- *That a file usually takes up a few more bytes than its size when it's saved.*
- *That you can cut, copy or paste a file or folder by right-clicking.*
- *How to select and copy, move or delete multiple files or folders.*
- *How to restore a file or folder that you deleted accidentally.*
- *How to identify and delete a shortcut.*
- *That this doesn't delete the file it points to.*

5.5 Making backups

If the hard disk in your computer fails or if the computer breaks down or is lost or stolen, you could lose all your files. These could include not only documents that you've worked on for weeks but also irreplaceable files such as your photos.

Your personal document files are usually all in *My Documents*, including sub-folders such as *My Pictures* and *My Music*. You can just drag *My Documents* to a thumbdrive, making a copy there. Safely remove the thumbdrive and store it away from the computer.

You could have dragged WP files to the desktop folder instead of leaving it in My Documents and putting a shortcut on the desktop. That's easier to do but its files wouldn't be backed up when you make a copy of My Documents.

If you have many photos or music files in *My Documents*, the copy of the folder may not fit on a thumbdrive. You can buy an external hard disk instead. It works exactly the same way as the thumbdrive but holds much more data.

Vista has folders called Pictures and Music instead of My Pictures and My Music. They are kept separately from Documents: you'll need to copy these as well to back them up.

If there's enough space on the external disk or thumbdrive, you can update the backup by renaming the old *My Documents* folder on it, copying the new version to it, then deleting the old version. If there isn't enough space to do this, you'll have to delete the old version before copying the new version. That's a bit riskier. Make absolutely sure you're deleting the backup *My Documents* and not *My Documents* on the computer itself!

You can use two external disks or thumbdrives so that one is always stored safely, even when you're updating files on the other one. Ideally, keep one of them in a different building in case of burglary or fire.

There are two different types of external hard disks available: ones that are powered from the computer and ones that have a separate power supply that needs to be plugged in. The ones with a separate power supply are generally less expensive but also less convenient.

If you use two thumbdrives or external disks and check once in a while that they're both working reliably, you can keep your documents and photos safe forever. They won't fade, crumble or get thrown away.

There are special programs available that you can use to manage backups. They save time because they only copy new and changed files to the backup.

There are services available that back up your files to a server on the Internet. They solve the problem of keeping the backup in a different building. However, if you have confidential information, are you sure no-one is going to snoop in the backup copy?

What you learned:

- What a backup is and why it's important to make one.
- That all that's normally needed is to make a copy of *My Documents* on a thumbdrive
- That you can use an external hard disk instead of a thumbdrive – it holds more.
- That it's a good idea to keep two backups and have one of them in a different building.
- *Why you should try to keep all your documents in the My Documents folder.*
- *That Vista keeps music and pictures separately from documents.*
- *That computer files and photos can outlast paper.*
- *That there are special programs for making backups which may be faster.*
- *That you can save your backups over the internet.*

5.6 The clipboard

You've used the clipboard to copy text and paste it somewhere else in a document and to cut or copy files and paste them in different folders.

The clipboard is part of Windows and every program can use it, including Word. As well as files, folders and text, it can hold other things such as pictures and spreadsheets as you'll see in Chapter 9. Because it's part of Windows, it can be used to move something from one program to another although only if the program you're pasting it into knows what to do with it.

For example, if you're looking at a web page using a browser program such as Internet Explorer or Firefox, you can select text or even a picture on the page, copy it and paste it into your Word document. If you have two documents open at once, you can cut or copy text from one document and paste it into the other one.

The clipboard only holds one thing at a time. When you copy something to it, it replaces whatever was there before.

6 Structuring a document

This chapter covers Word features that make it easier to type a document, format it consistently, give it a structure such as sections or chapters and add headers and footers and a table of contents. It covers additional features such as bullet points and numbered lists and discusses templates.

> By now, you should be quite familiar with drop down menus, dialogue boxes, etc. You won't need such detailed instructions and screenshots

6.1 Autocorrection

You need to make a new document containing some extracts from this book. Start Word as in Section 4.1 and type the following into the new document (press RETURN when you see ¶ and don't worry at all about formatting at this stage):

> Introduction¶
> Are you just starting with a computer to write letters?¶
> have

Word spotted that you're starting a new sentence but you didn't capitalise the *H* in *Have*. It's done that for you: this is its **auto-correction** feature. Sometimes it makes changes that you don't want. Just go back and undo the change it made – it'll get the hint. Continue typing:

> you been using a word processor for some time but still find it intimidating and feel that you don't understand what it's doing?¶
> If you fit either description, this book is meant for you.¶
> ¶
> Behind the screen¶
> "I'm buying a new computer. It has:¶
> An Intel Dual Core processor¶
> 4GB (232 bytes) of RAM"¶
> Chapters 2-5 of this book are general.¶
> ¶
> Basics of Windows¶
> This chapter covers basics such as managing program windows and switching between them.¶
> Maybe you already know this.¶
> Clicking with the mouse¶

> *Instead of using the left button, you can click with the right hand one. This has a different effect from normal clicking.¶*
> *It's possible to change settings so the mouse buttons are switched.¶*
> *Starting the Web Browser¶*
> *Click on Start at the bottom left of the screen.¶*
> *You'll see your choice of web browser program. Click on it.¶*

What you learned:

- **What auto-correction is and how to override it.**

6.2 Formatting individual characters

The text you typed in shows what 4GB is as a power of two but it needs to be formatted to make sense. Drag to select the second and third digits in *232*. Click *Format > Font....* A dialogue box appears. Click on the *Font* tab and tick *Superscript* under *Effects*. Click [OK]. The text is superscripted: the line reads *4GB (2^{32} bytes) of RAM"* which is correct.

> *You can also subscript characters, e.g. H_2O. The tabs in the dialogue box let you change other things including the colour of text and different styles of underlining. You see a preview of the selected text as you make changes. Explore the various options.*

What you learned:

- **How to create a superscripted character.**
- *How to subscript a character.*
- *How to change the colour of characters, etc.*

6.3 Numbering and bullets

Highlight part or all of the two paragraphs following *Introduction*. Remember that a new paragraph started when you pressed RETURN.

To the right of the buttons on the toolbar for text justification are buttons to turn numbering or bullets on and off. Tooltips help you to find them.

Click on the numbering button (≣). The lines become automatically numbered:

1. *Are you just starting with a computer to write letters?*
2. *Have you been using a word processor for some time but still*

> find it intimidating and feel that you don't understand what it's doing?

Click *Format > Bullets and Numbering....* The *Bullets and Numbering* dialogue box appears. Click the *Numbered* tab, then click on an alternative numbering style, e.g. *a) b) c)*. Click [OK]. The numbers are changed to letters.

> You could choose various other numbering styles including Roman numerals.

With the two paragraphs still selected, click ⁞≣ repeatedly. The letters appear and disappear. Leave them on.

Place the text cursor just after *doing?* and press RETURN:

a) Are you just starting with a computer to write letters?

b) Have you been using a word processor for some time but still find it intimidating and feel that you don't understand what it's doing?

c)

A letter appears and you could start typing a new lettered paragraph. Press CTRL+Z to undo this and get back to where you were.

Press SHIFT+RETURN. A new line starts and you could type another paragraph relating to item b). When you press RETURN again, item c) would open.

> Sometimes you need more than one paragraph under the same number or letter.

Press CTRL+Z to get back to where you were. Press RETURN, then BACKSPACE. The list is ended. You could start typing normal paragraphs with the same indentation as items in the list.

Press BACKSPACE again. You could start typing unindented paragraphs.

Press BACKSPACE a third time. It's as if you'd never pressed RETURN.

> This is confusing and you'll probably not remember how many times to press BACKSPACE. Just try to remember SHIFT+RETURN starts a new line in the current list item, pressing BACKSPACE once or twice exits the list with different

indentation and that, if you press BACKSPACE enough times, you can get rid of the last RETURN.

If you choose a multi-level numbering format in the Bullets and Numbering dialogue box (e.g. 1, 1.1, 1.1.1), you can change the level of list items by clicking ⇞ or ⇟. E.g. if you have a list with items 1, 2 and 3 and click on item 2, clicking ⇞ changes it to item 1.1. Item 3 becomes item 2.

Select the two paragraphs again and click on the bullets button (⋮≡). The numbers change to dots (**bullets**):

- Are you just starting with a computer to write letters?
- Have you been using a word processor for some time but still find it intimidating and feel that you don't understand what it's doing?

What you learned:

- **How to create a list of numbered or lettered items.**
- **How to add an item to the list.**
- **How to start a new line in an existing list item without it becoming a new list item.**
- **What a bullet is and how to create a list with them.**
- **How to end the list with different indents.**
- **How to change the numbering style, e.g. to Roman numerals.**
- **How to create a multilevel numbered list.**

6.4 Formatting paragraphs

Click to position the text cursor anywhere in the first line (*Introduction*).

To the left of the typeface selector box (saying e.g. *Times New Roman*) is the **paragraph style selector box**. Click on ⓐ to the left of that. The *Styles and Formatting* task pane appears to the right of the document. Make sure that the drop-down box at the bottom of the pane shows *Available Formatting*.

Instead of clicking ⓐ, you can click Format > Styles and Formatting....

Several different formatting styles are listed in the pane, including *Heading 1* and *Heading 2*. There should be a blue outline around *Normal*: this is because *Introduction* (like all of the document) is currently formatted in the *Normal* style.

Check that the text cursor is still in the first line, then click *Heading 1* in the *Styles and Formatting* pane. The whole line is given a different paragraph style suitable for a chapter title. Its typeface, style and size changes.

Right-click *Normal* in the *Styles and Formatting* pane and click *Modify*.... A dialogue box opens. Click [Format ▾] and click *Paragraph...* in the list that appears. A second dialogue box opens. Click the *Indents and Spacing* tab.

In the *Spacing* section of the tab, change the *Before* box from *0 pt* to *6 pt*. Click [OK] to close the second dialogue box and [OK] again to close the first one.

There's now extra space between all the Normal style paragraphs, making it easier to see where each one starts.

> *Changes to paragraph styles only affect the current document. When you start a new document, the styles will be as they were originally.*

Click its ✗ to close the *Styles and Formatting* pane.

Position the text cursor on the blank line above *Basics of Windows* and press DELETE.

> *We put a blank line to make it easier to spot the new chapter. It won't be needed any more.*

Make sure the cursor is on *Basics of Windows*. Click ▾ next to the style selector box (to the right of 44) and click on *Heading 1* in the drop-down list. The line changes to a chapter title like *Introduction*.

> *The paragraph style selector box lists the same styles as the Styles and Formatting pane. You can use it to apply them to other paragraphs without having to open the pane. Of course, when the pane is open, you can click the style there instead.*

Position the cursor in the line that reads *Clicking with the mouse* and click *Heading 2* in the style selector box. The line is given a style suitable for a subsection of a chapter. Repeat this with the line that reads *Starting the Web browser*.

What you learned:

- **That all paragraphs in a document are initially in Word's *Normal* style**
- **How to change individual paragraphs such as chapter titles to a different preset style.**
- **How to adjust one of Word's preset paragraph styles.**
- *That changes to paragraph styles only affect the current document.*

6.5 Numbering the chapters and sections

Click 🅰️ to open the Styles and Formatting pane, right-click *Heading 1* in the pane and click *Modify*.... Click [Format ▾] and click *Numbering...* in the list that appears. A dialogue box opens. Click the *Outline Numbered* tab. You see a choice of ways to number the chapters. Click the third choice from the left on the top row (1, 1.1, 1.1.1 with indents). Click [OK] to close the second dialogue box. The first box remains open.

Click [Format ▾] again but this time click *Paragraph...* in the list that appears. A different dialogue box opens. Click on the *Line and Page Breaks* tab. Tick *Page break before* and click [OK].

Tick *Automatically update* at the bottom right of in the first dialogue box. Click [OK].

The chapters and sections in the document are now numbered and each chapter starts on a new page.

> *Depending on the current view mode you may only see a dashed line marking the start of each new page.*
>
> *Several different modes can be selected in the View drop-down menu although you may need to click ✱ to see them all.*
> *Reading Layout can be useful sometimes but you'll usually want to select Normal Layout when you're making changes to a document.*

Triple-click or drag over any of the chapter headings to select it. Change the font size to 20 point. Notice that all the chapter headings become bigger.

> *This happened because you ticked Automatically update.*

When you set a paragraph to use a particular style, this doesn't prevent you from making other changes to the style of individual characters or words or even making changes to the style of the whole paragraph, e.g. by changing its justification or by clicking Format > Paragraph... and making other changes in the dialogue box. Unless the assigned style has Automatically update ticked, the changes won't affect other paragraphs using the same style.

This can cause problems: a paragraph may look odd or behave strangely in the table of contents because of some local formatting that you've forgotten about. You can remove all local formatting of a paragraph by selecting all of it, clicking Clear Formatting in the style selector box, then setting the required paragraph style again.

You'll often want to make tweaks to individual paragraphs of body text. It wouldn't be a good idea to tick Automatically update for the Normal style.

You can close the *Styles and Formatting* pane by clicking its ✕.

Click 🅰🅰 when you need to use the pane again.

Oops, we missed a chapter!

Position the cursor on the blank line above *Behind the screen* and press DELETE. Make sure the cursor is on *Behind the screen*. Choose *Heading 1* from the style selector box.

The line becomes the title for Chapter 2. *Basics of Windows* and its sections are automatically renumbered as Chapter 3.

What you learned:

- **That a change to a paragraph style immediately affects all the paragraphs of that style in the document. You don't have to find them all and change them one by one.**
- **That paragraphs of a particular style (e.g. chapter titles) can be automatically numbered.**
- **That the numbers update automatically when you make changes to the document.**
- *That different screen layouts for your document can be selected in the Views menu.*

6.5 Numbering the chapters and sections   **73**

- *That you'll usually want to select Normal Layout when editing a document.*
- *What Automatically update does and when to avoid using it.*
- *That you can still change the formatting of text and individual paragraphs.*
- *How to remove any formatting of an individual paragraph.*

6.6 Inserting a table

In Section 4.7 you saw how tab stops can be used to line up text in columns. You could use this to type a table in your document but Word has an easier and more powerful way.

Click at the end of the last line in Chapter 1 (*If you fit either description, this book is meant for you.*) and press RETURN.

Click *Table > Insert > Table....* A dialogue box opens. Set *Columns* to *4*. Click [OK]. A blank table is created with the cursor in the top left rectangle.

Type *Program* and press TAB. The cursor moves to the next box. Type *Formatting* and press TAB. Type *Styles* in the next box and *Grammar* in the last (top right) box. After you press TAB, the cursor should be in the left hand box on the second row. Type *Notepad* and press TAB.

> *When you're typing in a table, TAB moves to the next box to the right.*

Type *No, No* and *No* in the three boxes to the right of *Notepad*, pressing TAB after each *No*. A new blank row appears.

> *Notepad is a simple text editor included with Windows.*

Type *Libreoffice, Yes, Yes* and *No* in the four boxes in the new row.

Type *Word, Yes, Yes* and *Yes* in the four boxes of the next row.

Oops, two problems! You've got another blank row and you should have capitalised the *O* in *LibreOffice*.

Click *Table > Delete > Rows*. The unwanted blank row is deleted. Click on *Libreoffice* or use the arrow keys to move to it. Change the *o* to *O*.

Oops again! We forgot about WordPad. Click on *Notepad*. Click *Table > Insert > Rows Below*. A blank row is inserted between *Notepad* and *LibreOffice*. Type *WordPad, Yes, No* and *No* into it.

> WordPad is a simple word processor that's included with Windows. Although it can open Word documents, it struggles to display them properly and it can't save documents in Word format.

Move the mouse cursor outside the table to the left of *Program*. The cursor changes to a large arrow. Click. The whole first row of the table is selected. Click **B** or press CTRL+B. The selected words change to **bold**.

> You can select single or multiple entries in a table and change their justification, typeface, size and style just like any other text.

> The first row of the table shows the column headings. Right-click anywhere in the first row and click Table Properties... in the list that appears. A dialogue box opens. Click the Row tab, then click the tickbox to the left of Repeat as header row at the top of each page so that it's ticked. Click [OK]. This makes sure that, if the table won't all fit on one page, the first row will be repeated at the top of the part of the table on the next page.

> Drag to select all cells in the table, right-click, click Table Properties..., click on the Table tab in the Table Properties dialogue box, then click on [Borders and Shading...]. A dialogue box opens. Click on the Borders tab. You can change the style of lines around the selected cells. Choose None if you don't want any lines at all: this makes the table print out the same as it would if you'd used tab stops to set it up.

Click at the start of *Formatting* at the top left of the table and drag to after *Yes* at the bottom right. All of the last three columns are selected. Click ≡. The text in each selected cell is centred.

> If you place the cursor over the line between columns in the table, it changes to a line and arrows pointing side to side. You can drag it to change the width of the columns.

Click below the table. Click **B** or press the CTRL+B shortcut and type *Word Processor features*. Click ≡ to centre the caption.

> If you fit either description, this book is meant for you.

Program	Formatting	Styles	Grammar
Notepad	No	No	No
WordPad	Yes	No	No

6.6 Inserting a table

LibreOffice	Yes	Yes	No
Microsoft Word	Yes	Yes	Yes

Word Processor features

What you learned:

- How to insert a blank table.
- How to type text into the table.
- How to delete and insert rows in the table.
- How to edit text in the table.
- How to format text in the table.
- *What happens if the table won't fit on the current page.*
- *How to change the style of the lines in the table.*
- *How to adjust the width of the table columns.*

6.7 Adding a table of contents

Place the text cursor before the title of Chapter 1 (*Introduction*). Click on *Insert > Reference > Index and Tables....*

The *Insert Index/Table* dialogue box appears. Click on the *Table of Contents* tab. Note the *Show levels* box. Your document has levels *1* (chapters) and *2* (sections). So long as the box is set to *2* or higher, the table of contents will show both chapters and sections in each chapter. If you wanted to only show the chapters, you could set the box to *1*.

Click [OK]. The table is created. It shows the chapters and chapter sections in your document, complete with page numbers:

1	Introduction	2
2	Behind the Screen	3
3	Basics of Windows	4
	3.1 Clicking with the mouse	4
	3.2 Starting the Web Browser	4

> *You can mark words or phrases as entries for an alphabetic index by selecting one of them, pressing ALT+SHIFT+X and clicking* [Mark]. *While the dialogue box is open, you can select more words, clicking in Main entry: and pressing* [Mark] *again for each one. Close the dialogue box, click where you want the index to go and click Insert > Reference > Index and Tables.... Click on the Index tab, then on* [OK].

Chapter 6 Structuring a document

> *You can set up a cross-reference (e.g. See Page 1234) by clicking where you want the reference to point to. Click Insert > Bookmark.... A dialogue box opens. Give the bookmark a name that you'll recognise later, then click [Add]. Click where you want the cross-reference to appear and click Insert > Reference > Cross-reference.... Choose Bookmark as Reference type and click to select the bookmark you want. Under Insert reference to:, you can choose what to show: the page it's on or its paragraph number (if it has one) and/or whether it's above or below the cross-reference. Click [Insert] to add the cross-reference and click [Close] to close the dialogue box.*

The Table of Contents and any index and cross-references don't automatically update when you make changes to the document. They don't even update when you save and reopen it! To update them all, press CTRL+A to select everything in the document, then press the F9 key at the top of the keyboard.

> *The F1 to F12 keys are known as Function keys. With some keyboards, these keys have other functions too and only work as Function keys when the FN key is pressed or FN LOCK is enabled.*

What you learned:

- **How to create a table of contents.**
- **How quick and easy this is if you use paragraph styles and outline numbering.**
- **How to update the table of contents and any indexes and cross-references.**
- *How to create an index and cross-references.*
- *What the Function keys are.*

6.8 Giving the document a title

Click *File > Properties*. A dialogue box opens. Click on the *Summary* tab and type *Mini book* into the *Title* box.

> *You can set other information including the document's author on various tabs. This information, which doesn't appear in the document itself unless you insert it as a field, is known as **metadata**.*

Click on the *Statistics* tab. You see information about the document including a word count.

> *You can see the word count more easily by clicking Tools > Word Count.*

Click [OK].

What you learned:

- **How to set document meta-data, including a title.**
- **How to see statistics about the document, including a word count.**
- *What meta-data is.*

6.9 Adding a footer or header and fields

Click *View > Header and Footer*. A header box appears at the top and a footer box appears at the bottom of each page. A floating Header and Footer toolbar also appears.

> *You can drag the floating toolbar so it doesn't obscure what you're working on.*

Make sure the text cursor is in a footer box. Click *Insert > Field*.... A dialogue box appears. Choose *Document Information* in the *Categories:* box and click on *Title* in the *Field names:* below. Click [OK]. The book title (*Mini book*) appears in the footer.

Press TAB, then type *Page* and press SPACEBAR. Click [#] in the floating toolbar. Press SPACEBAR and type *of*. Press SPACEBAR again. Click [+] in the floating toolbar. The page number and total number of pages are shown.

> *You'll see that a Centred tab stop (⊥) was created automatically on the ruler so that the page numbers are centred in the footer. You can drag ⊥ off the ruler. This puts the title at the left side and the page numbers at the right.*

Look through the document. You'll see that there's a footer on each page showing the appropriate page number.

> *It's possible to include the chapter number and name in the footer but Word makes this cumbersome.*

You can put text and/or fields in the header at the top of each page instead of or as well as a footer.

The header and footer are both present all of the time but are only visible after View > Header and Footer is clicked. The sizes of the header and footer depend on what's in them. If there isn't anything there, they don't take up any space on the page.

Click *Close* in the floating toolbar. The toolbar disappears and the header and footer boxes may no longer be visible. However, if you click *View > Print Layout,* you'll see the document pages as they would be printed. Any headers and footers are visible in grey (but they would print in black).

What you learned:

- **How to add headers and footers to every page.**
- **How to use fields to insert information that's calculated or updated automatically.**
- **That the header and footer are there all the time but they are only visible in Print Layout view or after you click View > Header and Footer.**
- **That, although headers and footers are grey on the screen, they print normally.**

You won't be using the document again but you can save it for posterity if you want.

6.10 Templates

If you often make similar documents, for example if you need to write a monthly report, wouldn't it be nice to be able to start a new version with the paragraph styles and header or footer already set up? Not only would this save time, it would also help to keep new versions consistent in style with the previous ones.

When starting a new version, you could open a previous version, delete all the text that's not going to be needed in the new version, click *File > Save as...* to set the file name for the new version, then start typing the new text. This means having to delete a lot of stuff every time you start a new version of the document and there's the risk that you'll forget to rename it and lose the old version when you save the new one.

The better way is, after saving the document, to delete everything that won't be needed in future versions, then save it again as a **template** file. Click *File > Save As...* and choose *Document Template (*.dot)* as the file type.

> *Word usually saves its template files in the Application Data\Microsoft\Templates subfolder of your personal folder. This isn't inside your My Documents folder: the templates won't be backed up unless you back up Application Data too. To avoid this, you can click Tools > Options. A dialogue box opens. Click on the File Locations tab. Click on User Templates in the list so that it's highlighted, then click [Modify...]. Another dialogue box opens. Click on My Documents on the left hand side, then click [] at the top. Type in the name of the new templates folder (e.g. Templates), then click [OK] to close each of the dialogue boxes.*

> *If you already have template files in Application Data\Microsoft\Templates, you should move them to My Documents\Templates as described in Section 5.4. Remember that you need to start at My Computer to reach Application Data.*

> *Individual files and folders can be set to be **hidden** so that you don't normally see them. Application Data might be set this way. If you can't see it in your personal folder, click Tools > Folder Options.... A Dialogue box opens. Click the View tab and select the Show hidden files and folders radio button. Click [OK].*

> *You can choose any folder when you save a template file but Word doesn't seem to recognise that it's a template unless it's saved in the folder that's set under Tools > Options.*

When you want to make a new document based on a template, click *File > New....* A *New Document* task pane opens on the right-hand side. Under *Templates*, click *On my computer....* A selection box opens. Click the *General* tab. You should see your template. Click to select it, then click [OK].

Word knows that you've started a new document. When you click [] or *File > Save*, you'll be asked to give your document file a new name.

> *You can also start a new Office document by clicking [start], finding New Office Document and clicking on it. A dialogue box opens with many tabs. Most of these select groups of templates*

and wizards that are supplied with Office. You might want to look at these: they can get you started with many different tasks.

A **Wizard** guides you through some complicated procedure. Clicking on any wizard starts it. Clicking on a template opens a new document using it.

If you click on the General tab, you'll see your own templates.

What you learned:

- **When a template file is useful.**
- **How to prepare and save a template file.**
- **That, when you open a template file, Word knows you are starting a new document and will make sure you give it a name when you save it.**
- **How to change where Word keeps your templates so that they are backed up when you make a copy of My Documents.**
- **What a Wizard is.**
- **What hidden files and folders are and how to see them.**
- **How to start a document or wizard from New Office Document.**
- **That Office comes with templates and wizards for various tasks.**

7 Spreadsheets

Did you ever try to add up a column of numbers but got a different answer every time?

A spreadsheet is a powerful tool when you need to work with numbers. Not only does it do complicated calculations in a flash, it does them consistently and it records exactly how you set up the calculations for future reference.

This chapter is an introduction to the Excel spreadsheet.

Other spreadsheet programs are very similar.

7.1 Starting Excel

As in Section 4.1, click on [start], then move the mouse pointer over *All Programs*. A list appears. Move the mouse pointer over *Microsoft Office* in the list. Another list appears. Move the mouse pointer over *Microsoft Office Excel* and click.

The **spreadsheet** opens. It looks a bit like a table with columns and rows of **cells**. You'll notice the column headers: these identify each column with a different letter (*A*, *B*, *C*...). The rows are identified with numbers (*1*, *2*, *3*...). A cell can be specified by giving its column letter and row number. E.g. the top left cell is *A1*. Cell *B1* is to its right and cell *A2* is below it.

Click on cell *A1*. Its border is emphasised. Type *Ingredient* and press TAB. Cell *B1* is emphasised. Type *Amount* and press TAB. Cell *C1* is emphasised. Type *Price each* and press TAB. Cell *D1* is emphasised. Type *Cost*.

You might want to look at the screenshot below.

Click on cell *A2* (below *A1*) so its border is highlighted. Type *Flour (kg)* and press RETURN. Cell *A3* is emphasised. Type *Sugar (kg)* and press RETURN. Cell *A4* is highlighted. Type *Eggs*.

TAB moves to the next cell to the right. RETURN moves to the cell below. SHIFT+TAB moves to the cell to the left and SHIFT+RETURN moves to the cell above.

Type *0.5* in cell *B2*, *0.3* in cell *B3* and *2* in cell B4. Type *1.1* in cell *C2*,

1.8 in cell *C3* and *0.25* in cell *C4*.

Type *=B2*C2* in cell *D2* and press RETURN. *D2* shows *0.55*.

> A cell can contain text (words), a number or a **formula**. A formula starts with = and it can **refer** to other cells in the spreadsheet. In this case, the formula says to multiply together the numbers in cells B2 and C2 (amount and price), giving 0.55.
>
> A formula can contain numbers. In a formula, * multiplies, / divides and ^ raises to a power. For example, =6*2 would show 12, =6/2 would show 3 and =6^2 would show 36 (6 squared).

Click on cell *D2* and press CTRL+C. The formula is copied to the clipboard.

Drag the mouse cursor over cells *D3* and *D4*. Both cells are highlighted. Press CTRL+V. The formula is pasted into these cells.

Click in cell *D3*. You can see the formula it contains in the box at the top of the spreadsheet (circled below). It's *=B3*C3* rather than *=B2*C2* and the value of cell *D3* (*0.54*) is different from that of cell *D2*.

> When you paste a formula into a cell, any cells that it refers to are usually adjusted according to where the cell is relative to the original one. In Section 7.3 you'll see how to set an absolute reference where this doesn't happen.

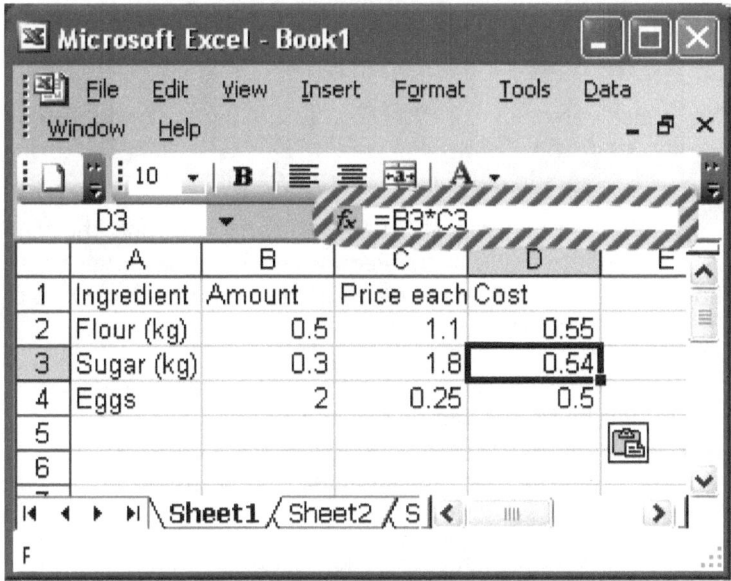

7.1 Starting Excel

Don't try making this cake. It'd probably be revolting!

What you learned:

- **What a spreadsheet cell is and how it's identified and referenced.**
- **That a cell can contain text, a number or a formula.**
- **That the value calculated by a formula is automatically shown in the cell.**
- **That the formula itself is shown in the box above the spreadsheet.**
- **That a formula can use the values of other cells (references).**
- **That a formula can be copied and pasted into additional cells.**
- **That, when this is done, any cell references in the formula are adjusted so they are relative to the new cell location.**
- *That you can use numbers as well as cell references in a formula.*
- *How to use TAB, RETURN and SHIFT to move to an adjacent cell.*

7.2 Using functions and inserting rows and columns

Click in cell *B6* and type *SUBTOTAL*. Click in cell *D6* and type *=sum(*. Don't press TAB or RETURN.

Drag the mouse cursor over cells *D2* to *D4*. They are highlighted. Type *)*. You see that the formula in cell *D6* is *=sum(D2:D4)*. Press RETURN. The value in cell *D6* is now *1.59*.

This formula uses Excel's built-in *SUM* function to add the values of cells *D2*, *D4* and any cells in between them. Dragging over these cells automatically puts the **cell range** into the formula. You could have typed it in as *D2:D4* instead.

> *Excel provides many other functions. For example, you can find the minimum, maximum or average value of a range of cells. Mathematical and trigonometric functions are available. Insert > Function... opens a dialogue box that helps you to find the function you need.*

Click *Help > Microsoft Excel Help*. The **Help** task pane appears on the right. Type *sum* into the *Search for:* box and press RETURN. Click on *SUM function* in the list of topics that appears in the pane. Information about the function is shown in a new window.

> *Microsoft Office, including Word, has a comprehensive though not always comprehensible help system. Try it for any other questions you have.*

The new window is separate from your document. You can resize, move and minimise it. Click on its ☒ to close it. Your document and the Help task pane remain open. You can close the task pane by clicking on its ✕.

> *Clicking Help > About Microsoft Office Excel opens a window with information including the exact version of the program that's installed. This is useful if you want to know if you have the newest version or need technical support. Most programs have similar Help menus.*

Click cell *B1*. Hold down SHIFT and click cell *D1*. The two cells along with *C1* are highlighted.

> *You can select multiple cells in the spreadsheet just like you select text (Section 4.6) or files in a folder (Section 5.4).*

> *Holding down CTRL lets you add a cell to an existing selection.*

> *Holding down SHIFT and clicking extends the selection by adding the new cell along with any cells in between.*

Click ≡. The contents of the selected cells become centred.

Click on the number *1* to the left of the top row of cells. The whole row is highlighted.

Click **B**. The contents of the highlighted cells are now in bold.

> *You can use the buttons and drop-down lists to change the typeface, size and style of cell contents, just as in Word.*

Click *Insert > Rows*. A new row of cells is added above the highlighted one.

Click cell *B2*. Hold down SHIFT and click cell *D7*. All the cells in rows *2-7* of columns *B*, *C* and *D* (a **rectangular area**) are highlighted. Place the mouse cursor over the dark outline around the selected cells so it changes to four arrows pointing in different directions. Drag the cells one column to the right.

You can insert rows or columns or drag a block of cells to make room for new entries.

References are automatically changed when rows or columns are inserted or cells are dragged. For example, the formula in cell E3 is =C3*D3. It was originally entered as =B2*C2 in cell D2.

What you learned:

- **How to use a built-in function in a formula.**
- **How to use the Microsoft Office Help menu.**
- **How to specify a range of cells or select them by dragging.**
- **How to select an entire row or column of cells.**
- **How to change the font (typeface, style and size) used to display cell contents.**
- **How to insert a row of blank cells.**
- **How to select cells in a rectangular area.**
- **How to move selected cells by dragging.**
- *That Excel has many built-in functions that you can find using Insert > Function....*
- *That references are automatically changed when you insert rows or columns or drag and drop cells.*
- *How to find the versions of Excel and other programs on your computer.*

7.3 Column widths and absolute references

Click cell *A1* and type *Cakes per batch*. Click cell *C1* and type *10*.

Click cell *B2*, type *Amount per cake* and press TAB.

Cell C2 is now highlighted. We want to change its contents from *Amount* to *Amount per batch*. Click after *Amount* in the box above the spreadsheet that shows the cell contents and press SPACEBAR. Type *per batch* and press RETURN. Cell C2 is updated.

Cakes per batch in cell *A1* is shown correctly even though it spills into cell *A2*. However *Amount per cake* and *Amount per batch* are truncated because the adjacent cells aren't blank. Place the mouse cursor between *B* and *C* above these columns. The cursor changes to a line with two arrows. Drag to the right. Column *B* becomes wider. Widen it enough so that *Amount per cake* is shown properly.

Repeat this procedure to widen column *C* so that *Amount per batch* is shown correctly.

> *You might also need to widen columns A and D slightly.*

Click cell *C3* and drag down to cell *C5*. Cells *C3*, *C4* and *C5* are highlighted. Press CTRL+C. Click on cell B3 and press CTRL+V. The contents of cells *C3-C5* are copied to cells *B3-B5*.

> *Moving instead of copying these cells would change the references to them in column E. We don't want that to happen.*

Click cell *C3*, type =c$1*b3 and press RETURN. Click cell *C3* again. Note that the letters *b* and *c* in the formula are automatically changed to *B* and *C* – you don't need to press SHIFT when typing references or function names in a formula.

Press CTRL+C. Highlight cells *C4* and *C5* and press CTRL+V.

> *Note that the values shown in cells C3-C5 are all 10 times larger than the numbers in cells B3-B5.*

If you click on cells C3, C4 and C5 in turn, you'll see that the formulas are =*C$1*B3*, =*C$1*B4* and =*C$1*B5* respectively. The *$* in *C$1* made it an **absolute reference** telling the spreadsheet to always refer to the cell in row *1*, even when the formula is pasted into other cells lower (or higher) in the same column.

> *If you wanted to paste the formula into cells in different columns, you could put $ in front of the letter in the reference. E.g. the formula =C1*B3 would always refer to cell C1 no matter where it was pasted into the spreadsheet.*

What you learned:

- **How to modify the contents of a cell.**
- **How to change the width of a column.**
- **How to specify an absolute reference to another cell that doesn't change when the formula is copied and pasted.**
- **That you don't have to press SHIFT when you type a cell reference.**

7.4 Calculations, currencies and merged cells

Click cell *B9*. Type *Mark-up* and press TAB. Click % on the Excel toolbar, type *76* and press TAB twice. Type *=e7*c9* and press RETURN.

> *You've formatted cell C9 as a **percentage** and set it to 76. Excel shows this as 76% and the actual value of the cell becomes 0.76 (76/100).*

Click cell *B10* and type *Batch Price*. Click cell *E10* and type = (don't press TAB or RETURN). Click cell *E7*, type + *and* click cell *E9*. The formula shows as *=E7+E9*. Press RETURN.

> *When you're entering or editing cell contents, you can insert a reference to another cell by clicking on it.*

Click on cell *B11* and type *Postage*. Click on cell *E11* and type *5*.

Click on cell *B12* and type *Price per cake*. Click on cell *E12* and type *=e11+e10/c1*. Press RETURN.

Cell E12 shows *7.7984* but that's plainly wrong. The batch price plus postage is just over £30 so the cost per cake should be about £3, not almost £8.

> *It's always a good idea to look at the result of a calculation to see if it looks plausible.*

This error happened because Excel calculates values from formulas using algebraic conventions. Multiplications and divisions are done before additions and subtractions. Excel is dividing the batch price (*E10*) by the number of cakes, then adding the whole postage charge (*E11*). You need to add brackets (parentheses) so that Excel does the addition before the division.

Click on cell *E12*. Click after = in the formula in the box above the spreadsheet and type *(*. Press the right arrow key repeatedly until the cursor is just before / in the formula. Type *)* and press RETURN. The price is now 3.2984.

> *When you're editing cell content, the left and right arrow keys move the cursor backwards and forwards. At other times, they change your position in the spreadsheet.*

The costs and prices are a bit of a mess. Surely they should be in pounds and whole pence (or dollars or Euros and whole cents)?

Click on the letter *D* above the third column of cells. The whole column is highlighted. Hold down CTRL and click on the letter *E* at the top of the fourth column. Both columns are now highlighted.

Click *Format > Cells*. A dialogue box appears. Click on the *Number* tab. Click on *Currency* in the *Category* box, then click [OK]. All numbers in columns *C* and *D* are now formatted as **currency** amounts. The way they appear depends on your location settings: they will usually show the symbol for your local currency and the appropriate number of digits of minor units (e.g. 2 digits for pence or cents).

> *The price per cake is now shown as £3.30 instead of 3.2984. Excel rounds the amount to the nearest penny.*

Click on the number *1* to the left of the top row of cells and click *Insert > Rows*. A new row of cells is added above the highlighted row.

Select the new cells *A1* to *E1*. Click ▦ (to the right of the text justification buttons). Cells *A1* to *M1* are merged into one. Click in the merged cell, type *CAKE PRICE CALCULATION* and press RETURN.

Select cells *B4* to *B6* (e.g. by dragging). Hold down CTRL and select cells D4 to D6. While still holding down CTRL, click on cells *C2*, *C10* and *E12*. You've selected all the cells with numbers (rather than text or formulas) in them. Release CTRL and click **B**.

> *Numbers that you might want to twiddle later are now in **bold**.*

What you learned:

- What happens when you format a cell as a percentage.
- That you can enter a cell reference in a formula by clicking on the cell.
- That the order of calculations follows algebraic conventions.
- That you can use brackets (parentheses) to change the order of calculations in a formula.
- That you can use the left and right arrow keys when you're editing a formula.
- That you can add cells to an existing selection by holding down CTRL.
- How to format cells so they show their values as currency amounts.
- How to merge cells when you need more space.
- *That you can use the four arrow keys to move around the spreadsheet.*
- *That values are automatically rounded (e.g. to pence) when shown as a currency.*

7.5 Saving the spreadsheet

Click 💾. A dialogue box appears which is similar to the one you see when saving a Word document.

As with Word, type the file name, e.g. *Cakes*. Click [Save].

> *A spreadsheet can be saved as a template. Choose Save as type: Template (*.xlt).*

What you learned:

- **How to save a spreadsheet file.**
- *That the spreadsheet can be saved as a template.*

7.6 Using the spreadsheet

You can change any of the numbers (formatted in bold) and the spreadsheet updates immediately. You can change the number of cakes per batch, the amount or cost of each ingredient, the mark-up percentage or the postage and see the effect.

> *If you change numbers in the spreadsheet just to see what happens, you'll be asked whether to save your changes when you close Excel. Provided that you saved the spreadsheet before you started twiddling the figures and you don't want to save the latest figures you entered, you can click [No].*

What you learned:

- **That the whole spreadsheet is updated immediately when you change any value in it.**

8 Charts and Sorting

This chapter covers some more advanced spreadsheet functions including handling dates, sorting rows and making charts (graphs).

The spreadsheet you make in this chapter will also be used in Chapters 9 and 11.

Start Excel. A new spreadsheet opens. Fill in cells *A1* to *C11* with data as follows:

	A	B	C
1	**Title**	**First name**	**Surname**
2	Mr	Riley	Holt
3	Mr	Zachary	Vincent
4	Mrs	Chloe	Vincent
5	Ms	Elise	Gill
6	Mr	Kieran	Kirby
7	Mr	Taylor	Bevan
8	Mrs	Tilly	North
9	Mr	Ellis	Holt
10	Miss	Faith	Bibi
11	Mr	Andrew	Holland

Fill in cells D1 to F11 as follows:

	D	E	F
1	**Address**	**Town**	**Postcode**
2	52 Asfordby Rd	ALDBROUGH	DL11 5DL
3	58 Netherpark Cr	STETCHWORTH	CB8 0HZ
4	79 Essex Rd	TARBERT	HS3 4RC
5	92 Gloddaeth St	BIRCHAM TOFTS	PE31 0OR
6	89 Sandyhill Rd	GAER	NP8 3FJ
7	59 Western Tce	MISERDEN	GL6 4OR
8	46 Hindhead Rd	EARDINGTON	WV16 1CO
9	22 Circle Way	CAERAU	CF34 5YN
10	25 Trinity Cr	WHEEDLEMONT	AB54 8HC
11	63 Ivy Lane	WARDGATE	DE6 5II

Fill in cells *G1* to *I11* as follows:

	G	H	I
1	**Born**	**Height**	**Weight**
2	2/11/40	188	112.1
3	2/4/28	170	88.9
4	9/4/78	156	50.6
5	8/4/81	166	62.4
6	11/8/49	179	109.5
7	9/3/69	170	66.7
8	7/3/43	174	98.4
9	12/5/46	173	84
10	1/6/42	170	59
11	4/12/72	187	87.3

The whole table wouldn't fit in the book: that's why it's in three chunks.

Dates are deliberately chosen so that they appear valid in either American (m/d/y) or European (d/m/y) format. Heights are in centimetres and weights in kilograms.

You might notice that Mr. Vincent is shown as being born in 2028. Leave this as it is.

Select cells *A1* to *L11* so that they are highlighted. Click *Format > Column > AutoFit Selection*. The column widths are adjusted automatically to suit the selected cells.

Click ⊞ and save the spreadsheet as *People*.

You don't want to have to type all that stuff in again if something goes wrong.

What you learned:

- That a spreadsheet can be used to make a simple table of data (e.g. names and addresses).
- How tedious it can be to type in names and addresses.
- How to get Excel to automatically adjust column widths.

8.1 Making an x-y (scatter) chart

Are the heights and weights of people in this table related?

Drag to select cells *I4* and *I5*. Put the mouse cursor over the outline and drag the cells to *J4* and *J5*. Select cell *I8*, put the mouse cursor over its outline and drag it to *J8*. Select cell *I10* and drag it to *J10*.

Now the men have their weights in column *I* and the women's weights are in column *J*. Change cell *I1* to *Men* and cell *J1* to *Women*.

Drag to select cells *H1* to *J11*. Click *Insert > Chart....* The **Chart Wizard** appears. Make sure the *Standard Types* tab is selected.

Click on Chart type *X-Y (scatter)* to select it. Click [Next >] twice, then click on the *Titles* tab. Type *Height (cm)* into the *X axis* box and *Weight (kg)* into the *Y axis* box. Click [Finish]. The chart is created.

Position the mouse cursor just inside the rectangular black outline around the chart and drag it down and to the left until its top left covers cell A13.

Notice that the minimum height is over 150 cm. Right-click on the numbers for the X (Height) axis and choose *Format axis....* A dialogue box opens. Click on the *Scale* tab and enter *150* in the *Minimum:* box. Click [OK].

> *The variation in height is now easier to see.*

The X-Y chart is now nicely set up. There's a dot for each person. Its horizontal position shows their height and its vertical position shows their weight. It shows that the men are generally taller than the women and that the taller people tend to be heavier.

> *Scandal! These people don't really exist. The data you're using is completely fake and has been chosen to make the chart look plausible.*

It would be interesting to see these people's *Body Mass Index*.

Click cell *K1* and type *BMI*. Click cell *K2* and type *=10000*i2/h2^2*.

> *Body Mass Index is the person's weight in kilograms divided by the square of their height in metres. The ^2 tells Excel to square the value of H2. You need to multiply by 10,000 (100^2) because the heights are recorded in centimetres rather than metres.*

Copy the formula in cell *K2* into cells *K3-11*.

There's a problem: the women's weights are in a different column and their BMIs are shown as zero. Click on an incorrect cell, then on the formula in the box at the top. Cells in column *H* and *I* are highlighted in different colours, indicating that they are used in the formula. Put the mouse cursor over the outline of the highlighted cell in column *I* and drag it across to column *J*. Press RETURN. The BMI is now correct.

Repeat to fix the BMIs for the other three women.

The BMI values are ridiculously precise. Select cells K2 to K11 and click *Format > Cells...*. A dialogue box appears. Click on the *Number* tab and choose *Number* under *Category:*. Under *Negative numbers:*, click on -1234.10. Change *Decimal places* from *2* to *1*. Click [OK]. The BMI values are rounded to one digit after the decimal point, e.g. 30.8 for Mr. Vincent instead of 30.761246.

> *Rounding set in Format > Cells only affects the values when they are shown. It doesn't affect the results of formulas elsewhere that refer to those cells. E.g. if you enter =K3 as a formula in cell L3 and format it with 6 decimal places, you'll see 30.761246 there. If you wanted to round the value in references to 1 decimal place too, you could use =round(10000*i2/h2^2, 1) as the formula in K2.*

What you learned:

- **What an X-Y (scatter) chart is and how to create one.**
- **How to add captions to the chart axes.**
- **How to move the chart.**
- **How to change the minimum value for a chart axis.**
- **That cell references in a formula can be changed by dragging.**
- **How to format cells to show a different number of digits after the decimal point.**
- *That this doesn't affect the value of the cell, only the way it's shown.*
- *That you can use the built-in ROUND() function to round a value in or result of a formula.*

8.2 Date and time calculations

> *The normal range for BMI is 18.5 to 25. Some of the people are overweight. We'll calculate their ages and see if "middle age spread" is the problem.*

Click on cell *K1*. Click *Insert > Columns*. A new column is inserted. Type *Age* into the new blank cell *K1*. Type *=now()-g2* into cell *K2* and press RETURN.

You see a meaningless date and time in *K2*. With *K2* selected, click *Format > Cells...*. On the *Number* tab, set *Category* to *number*, *Format* to *-1234.10*, *Decimal places* to *0* and click [OK]. The cell now shows a huge number which is still pretty meaningless.

Change the formula in cell *K2* to *=int((NOW()-G2)/365.25)* and press

RETURN. The cell shows Mr. Holt's age correctly.

The NOW() function gives the current date and time when the cell is edited or a saved spreadsheet is opened. The date and time is in days since the start of 31 December 1899: the fractional part gives the time of day. For example, midday on 1 January 1900 is represented by the number 1.5.

If a cell contains something that looks like a date and/or time, Excel automatically converts it to a number and formats the cell so that it interprets the number in a format similar to what you entered (it may not be exactly the same). When you enter a time without a date, it's converted to a number between 0 and 1, as if it was that time on 31 December 1899. When you enter a date without a time, it's converted to a whole number as if the day had just started.

You can tell Excel to display any number as if it's a date and/or time of day. There's a wide choice of formats on the Numbering tab.

You can add or subtract cells containing dates and times, e.g. to see how much time has elapsed between two dates and times or when some number of days will have elapsed. No need to account for how many days there are in each month.

We want the ages in years rather than days so we need to divide by the number of days in a year. We're using 365.25 days to account for leap years.

We also want to see the person's age at their last birthday. If someone is 29 years and 8 months old, we want to see 29, not 29.67 or 30 (which is 29.67 rounded to the nearest whole number). The INT() function rounds numbers down.

The result will still be wrong very occasionally because of our simplification of leap years.

You might input something that Excel thinks is a date or time, and tries to convert when it shouldn't. For example, suppose you note the terms of a loan by typing APR 10 into a cell. Excel interprets this as a date. You can prevent this or other attempts to interpret a text string as a number or formula by starting it with a single quote, e.g. 'APR 10.

Copy the formula in cell *K2* into cells *K3-K11* so that everyone's age is shown.

Oops! Mr. Vincent's age is negative!

> *When you enter a date with a two digit year (e.g. 2/4/28), Excel guesses the century. It normally uses a cut-off year of 1930: years 30-99 are in the 20th century (1930-1999) while years 00-29 are in the 21st century (2000-2029). It thinks Mr. Vincent isn't born yet.*

Click cell *G3* and enter the date of birth as *2/4/1928*. His age is now correct.

What you learned:

- **How Excel records, calculates and shows dates and times.**
- **That Excel can't always correctly interpret years entered as two digits.**
- *How to determine the current date and time.*
- *How to round down a calculation result.*
- *How to display dates and times in the way you want.*
- *How to calculate elapsed times or when a time will have elapsed.*
- *How to tell Excel that a string is text and not to try to interpret it.*

8.3 Making a column chart

Select cells *K1* to *L11*. Click *Insert > Chart....* The Chart Wizard appears again. Chart type *Column* should already be selected: if not, click on it. Click [Finish]. The chart is created. Position the mouse cursor just inside the rectangular black outline of the new chart and drag it down so it's to the right of the X-Y chart.

> *The chart shows the ten people in order with two bars for each person. One indicates their age and the other indicates their BMI. There might be a relationship but it isn't at all clear.*

Select cells *A2* to *L11*. Click *Data > Sort....* A dialogue box appears. Set the *Sort by* box to *Age*. Leave the other two boxes blank. Click [OK].

> Be sure to select all the columns required before sorting data. If you miss some out, they'll be left unchanged and will become associated with the wrong records.

The selected rows are sorted by increasing age and the chart updates automatically.

> When you choose a column for sorting, it can contain numeric values or text. Text is sorted alphabetically. For example, you could choose Sort by Surname but there are two people with the surname Holt and two with Vincent. You could choose First name as the first Then by so that people with the same surname are sorted by their first name. For each column you choose, you can reverse the sort order (e.g. 10 to 1 or Z to A) by clicking the Descending radio button.

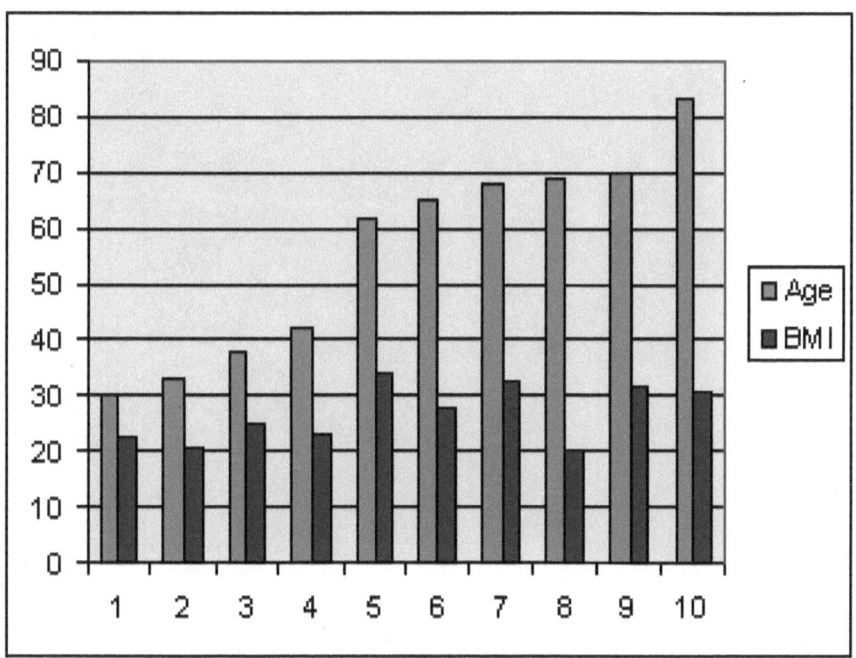

> The chart shows some slight evidence of middle age spread. A lot more people would have to be added before we could say for sure.

Be sure to click 💾 to update the saved spreadsheet. You'll be using it again.

8.3 Making a column chart

We've only briefly touched on the different types of chart and the ways to smarten them up. There are a great many options that can be set in the Chart Wizard and charts can be modified after they have been created. You may want to experiment.

What you learned:

- **What a column chart is and how to make one.**
- **How to quickly sort data stored in an Excel spreadsheet.**
- *That you can select a text column to sort data alphabetically.*
- *To be careful when selecting the columns to be sorted.*
- *That there's a lot more you can learn about charts.*

9 Graphics and Pages

In this chapter, you'll use Word to write a report based on what you found out in Chapter 8. The report will include the charts from the spreadsheet and will show the raw data as an embedded spreadsheet that looks like a table when it's printed.

This chapter may be most useful to students.

9.1 Pasting graphics and data from the spreadsheet

Start Excel and go to the *File* drop-down menu. You'll see the names of recently used spreadsheet files. If *People.xls* (the spreadsheet you made in Chapter 8) is there, click on its name to open it.

If you've used several other spreadsheets since *People.xls*, it may not be listed there any longer. You can open it from *File > Open* or just close Excel, click [start], go to *My Documents* and open it.

> *Word has the same feature for opening recently-used documents. You can also open any recent document by clicking* [start]*, moving the cursor over My Recent Documents and clicking the document in the list that appears.*

Leaving the spreadsheet open, start Word. A new document opens.

Both the new Word document and the *People* spreadsheet are in your computer's RAM and Word and Excel are multitasking (Section 3.3). You can switch between them by clicking their buttons on the taskbar (the new Word document should be called something like *Document1*). Switch back to the *People* spreadsheet.

> *You can also switch programs and documents by holding down the ALT key and pressing TAB. The first time you press TAB, you'll see all your documents and any open folders in a box in the middle of the screen. One of them will have a square around it. Each time you press TAB again, the square moves to the next document or folder. When it's around the one you want, release ALT.*

Click just inside the rectangle around the X-Y chart of weight versus height that you made in Section 8.1. It becomes selected and 8 small black squares appear around it. Press CTRL+C to copy it to the clipboard.

Click on your new untitled Word document on the taskbar or use ALT+TAB to switch to it. It reappears. Press CTRL+V and press RETURN. The X-Y chart is pasted into the document with the text cursor below it.

Switch back to the *People* spreadsheet. Click just inside the rectangle around the column chart of ages and BMIs that you made in Section 8.3 and copy it to the clipboard.

Switch to the new Word document, make sure that the text cursor is flashing below the X-Y chart (click below the chart if it isn't) and press CTRL+V, then RETURN. The column chart is pasted into the document.

Switch to the *People* spreadsheet. Select cells *B1* to *L11* (a rectangular area) and press CRTL+C to copy it to the clipboard.

Switch to the new Word document, make sure the text cursor is flashing below the column chart and press CTRL+V. The selected cells are pasted into the document as a table. Press RETURN.

What you learned:

- **Two ways to see and quickly open documents you worked on recently.**
- **A situation where it's useful to have two programs running at the same time.**
- **How to paste charts from a spreadsheet into a Word document.**
- **How to paste part of a spreadsheet into a Word document as a table.**
- *How to use ALT+TAB to switch between open documents.*

9.2 Portrait, Landscape and paper size

Click *View > Print Layout*. You'll see that there's a problem: the table is too wide to fit on the page.

Place the mouse cursor outside the table to the left of the top row (the headings). It changes to a large arrow. Drag down to underneath the table at the middle so that it's all selected, including the blank line below it.

Click *File > Page Setup....* The *Page Setup* dialogue box opens. On the *Margins* tab under *Orientation*, click A (above *Landscape*). Set the

Apply to: box lower down to read *Selected text*. Click [OK].

> Common paper sizes such as A4 (210 x 297 mm) and Letter (8½ x 11 inch) aren't square. Portrait orientation puts the shorter side at the top while landscape orientation puts the longer side there. Think of paintings of a person (**portrait**) or a scene (**landscape**) in an art gallery.
>
> You don't need to change the way that the paper is loaded into the printer when you print a landscape page. The computer automatically rotates the image of the page when it sends it to the printer.
>
> You can click the Paper tab in the Page Setup dialogue box and change the page size for your document. Usually, this should match the size of the paper loaded into the printer.
>
> The **printer driver** installed in Windows to control the printer needs to know the size of the paper. You can set this after clicking File > Print... by clicking [Properties] next to the printer selection.
>
> If the document page and printer paper sizes differ, options depend on your particular printer and can't be covered in detail here. Possibilities include:
>
> - Printing the page normal size with blank space or bits missing.
> - Shrinking or enlarging the page to fit the paper.
> - Printing each large page on several smaller sheets of paper that you stick together afterwards (**tiling**).
> - Printing multiple pages on each sheet of paper, e.g. two A5 portrait pages side by side on an A4 landscape sheet.
> - Showing an error message or flashing indicator light.
>
> Your printer might be able to print on both sides of the paper (**duplex printing**). If not, you can print one side, reload the printed sheets and print the other side: this involves some trial and error.

The table is now on a second page that's landscape oriented. It's wide enough for the table to fit.

Word saw that it had to put the table on a new page because the orientation had changed. You can change subsequent pages back to portrait orientation the same way: start where you want the change to happen, select everything below there, click File > Page Setup..., choose Portrait orientation and Selected text, then click [OK].

If you want an entire document to be in Landscape mode, choose Apply to: Whole document in the Page Setup dialogue box.

What you learned:

- **How to change the orientation of pages from Portrait to Landscape.**
- *What Portrait and Landscape pages are.*
- *How to change subsequent pages back from Landscape to Portrait orientation.*
- *How to change an entire document to Landscape orientation.*
- *How to change page and paper sizes.*
- *What might happen if the sizes don't match.*
- *Two ways to print on both sides of the paper.*

9.3 Pasting a spreadsheet

The table we pasted into the new document would be quite adequate but we'll do something a bit more advanced...

Switch back to the *People.xls* spreadsheet, make sure cells *B1* to *L11* are still selected and press CTRL+C.

Switch to the new Word document and click below the table on the second page. Click *Edit > Paste Special...*. A dialogue box opens.

You'll see that *HTML Format* is highlighted in the list. Click on *Microsoft Office Excel Worksheet Object* to highlight it instead. Make sure that the radio button next to *Paste:* on the left is selected, then click [OK]. After a short delay, a slightly different second copy of the table appears. Press RETURN twice so the cursor is below the table.

The new copy isn't just a table. Double-click on it. It turns into a little spreadsheet with its own scrollbars (arrowed below) **embedded** in the

Word document.

	B	C	D	E	F	G	H	I	J	K	L
1	First na	Surnam	Address	Town	Postcod	Born	Height	Men	Women	Age	BMI
2	Elise	Gill	92 Gloddaeth St	BIRCHAM TOF	PE31 0OR	08/04/1981	166		62.4	30	
3	Chloe	Vincent	79 Essex Rd	TARBERT	HS3 4RC	09/04/1978	156		50.6		
4	Andrew	Holland	63 Ivy Lane	WARDGATE	DE8 5II	04/12/1972	187	87.3		39	25.0
5	Taylor	Bevan	59 Western Toe	MISERDEN	GL6 4OR	09/03/1969	170	66.7		42	23.1
6	Kieran	Kirby	89 Sandyhill Rd	GAER	NP8 3FJ	11/08/1949	179	109.5		62	34.2
7	Ellis	Holt	22 Circle Way	CAERAU	CF34 5YN	12/05/1946	173	84		65	28.1
8	Tilly	North	46 Hindhead Rd	EARDINGTON	WV16 1CO	07/03/1943	174		98.4	68	32.5
9	Faith	Bibi	25 Trinity Cr	WHEEDLEMON	AB54 8HC	01/06/1942	170		59	69	20.4
10	Riley	Holt	52 Asfordby Rd	ALDBROUGH	DL11 5DL	02/11/1940	188			71	31.7
11	Zachary	Vincent	58 Netherpark C	STETCHWORTH	CB8 0HZ	02/04/1928	170	88.5		83	30.8

Sheet1 / Sheet2 / Sheet3 /

The drop-down menus above the document change to Excel ones when the spreadsheet opens. You'll be using the little black squares (circled) in Section 9.7.

When you click Edit > Paste or press CTRL+V, Word pastes whatever is on the clipboard into your document in what it thinks is the way you're most likely to want. Edit > Paste Special... shows you the different ways that the paste can be done and lets you choose. Unfortunately the names of the different choices can be obscure.

*There are three basic ways something might be pasted. The most advanced and powerful is as an embedded object like this spreadsheet. The second option is as **formatted text** – it looks much as it did where it came from but it may not have all the functions that it originally had. HTML Format is an example of this: it's what Word chose when you pressed CTRL+V and it pasted the spreadsheet cells as a table.*

*The third way is as **unformatted text**. This puts whatever is on the clipboard into the document as if you'd just typed it in, without keeping formatting such as its original font. For example, if you find some useful information on a web page and you want to paste it into a document that's already formatted, you don't want the pasted text to be in the web designer's choice of font.*

Change cell *I1* to read *Weight* instead of *Men*. Select cells *J2* and *J3* and drag them to *I2* and *I3*. Select cells *J8* and *J9* and drag them to *I8* and *I9*. All the weights are now in column *I*.

Click on the letter *J* above column *J* and click *Edit > Delete*. The column disappears.

9.3 Pasting a spreadsheet

You can select several columns at once or select rows instead of columns and click Edit > Delete to get rid of them.

If you select a cell or range of cells that don't make up a whole row or column and click Edit > Delete Cells, you'll see a dialogue box where you can choose whether to delete just the selected cells and move the cells in all rows below up to fill the space or move the cells in all columns to the right leftwards. You can also choose to delete the rows or columns containing the selected cells entirely.

If you want to delete the cell contents but leave the blank cells in place, you can click Edit > Clear > All. You can also delete only certain elements, e.g. formatting such as bold that you've applied to the cells.

Look at the X-Y chart you pasted in at the top of the page. It still shows men and women separately. The chart is just a copy. It's no longer linked to either People.xls or to the part of People.xls pasted separately into the Word document. It won't update.

Click on cell *G11* and retype the date as *2/4/28*. Press RETURN. Mr. Vincent's age in cell *J3* is negative again. Press CTRL+Z to undo this change.

The embedded spreadsheet updates when you change data, just like the original one.

Click below the embedded spreadsheet. It closes: it's now just columns of text, etc.

The headings probably won't be visible and the column widths might need adjustment. We'll fix those soon.

What you learned:

- **How to embed part of a spreadsheet into a Word document.**
- **That you can edit the embedded spreadsheet just as if you were using Excel.**
- **That the embedded spreadsheet updates just as if you were using Excel.**
- **How to delete a column from a spreadsheet.**
- **How to close an embedded spreadsheet.**

- *How to delete multiple columns or rows or a range of cells from a spreadsheet.*
- *How to selectively delete the contents of cells, leaving the cells themselves in place.*
- *How to paste text into your document without bringing along its formatting.*
- *That spreadsheet cells and charts pasted separately are no longer linked.*

9.4 Inserting pictures

Switch to the *People* spreadsheet. Hold down the ALT key and press the small key marked *Print Scrn*. It's usually near the top right of the keyboard and may have a slightly different label. A screenshot is made of the spreadsheet window and it's put on the clipboard.

> *Pressing ALT+Print Scrn copies the current active window to the clipboard. Pressing Print Scrn on its own copies the whole screen, including all visible windows and the taskbar.*

Switch to the new Word document, click below the embedded spreadsheet and press CTRL+RETURN. A new page is started with the text cursor at its top. Press CTRL+V. The screenshot is pasted into the Word document.

> *This may not work correctly due to a bug in Word. If this happens, press CTRL+Z, then click Edit > Office Clipboard.... The task pane to the right of your document shows items that you've pasted into your document. The top item is the current content of the clipboard. Click on it.*

> *The screenshot is a picture: it's as if you'd used a digital camera to photograph your computer's screen. Instead of pasting, you could click Insert > Picture > From file... and choose any picture (e.g. a photograph) that's stored on your computer.*

> *Instead of pasting the screenshot directly into your document, you could start a picture editing program such as Paint (included with Windows) and paste it there. Then you could make changes such as cropping it to remove bits you don't want or adding circles around things as you've seen in this book. You can then either save it as a file and use Insert > Picture > From*

> *file... or copy it back to the clipboard and paste it into your document.*
>
> *Paint is a very simple program without many facilities. You can buy much better programs such as Adobe Photoshop or you can try the free open-source GIMP. Type GIMP into a search engine, find the Windows version and download and install it. Unfortunately GIMP, although very powerful, can't be described as user-friendly.*

Click on the screenshot and press BACKSPACE twice. It disappears along with the third page. You saw how to insert them but we don't want them.

> *Insert > Picture > From file... puts a copy of the picture into your document. Moving, changing or deleting the original file doesn't affect the copy. Removing the picture from the document deletes the copy but doesn't affect the original file.*

Click on the table above the embedded spreadsheet and click *Table > Delete > Table*. The table disappears: we don't want that either.

> *If you tried to use BACKSPACE or DELETE to get rid of the table, it would only affect letters in it. Even if you select all the text in the table and press DELETE, the empty table remains.*

What you learned:

- **How to start a new page by pressing CTRL+RETURN.**
- **How to copy a screenshot to the clipboard.**
- **How to paste a screenshot into a Word document.**
- **How to remove a screenshot or picture from the document.**
- **How to delete a table in the document.**
- *How to insert a picture or photograph on your computer into the document.*
- *That inserting a picture or photograph makes a new copy that's part of the document.*
- *That you can edit screenshots or other pictures before you put them in your document.*
- *That you can use Paint to do this but other programs are more powerful.*

- *How to find, download and install an open-source Windows program.*

9.5 Formulas

You might need to put a mathematical formula or equation into a document, e.g. the quadratic equation $\dfrac{-b \pm \sqrt{b^2 - 4ac}}{2a}$. Click *Insert > Object...*. A dialogue box opens. On the *Create New* tab, choose *Microsoft Equation*. Click [OK]. An equation object is inserted and you can edit it using its floating toolbar. Details are beyond the scope of this book but you can click *Help > Equation Editor Help Topics*.

9.6 Sizing and anchoring graphics

Click to the right of the column chart on the first page. Press CTRL+* to show non-printing characters. Press RETURN twice, then LEFT ARROW once.

> This separates the text cursor from the Section Break so that text appears correctly in Normal view mode as you type it in.

Select *Normal* in the paragraph style selector box. Type (pressing RETURN each time you see ¶):

What shape are you?¶
¶
I compared the height and weight of ten people. This chart shows what I found.¶
¶
The women are generally shorter although the taller women are taller than the shortest men.¶
¶
Taller people, both women and men, generally weigh more than shorter ones.¶
¶
This chart shows the age and Body Mass Index of the ten people.¶
¶
There's very little sign here that Body Mass Index varies with age.

Click on *What shape are you?*. Select *Heading 1* in the paragraph style selector box and click ≡. The heading is centred.

Click on the X-Y chart of weight versus height that you pasted at the start of the document. You'll see black squares at its corners and in the middle of each side. These are **handles**. Place the mouse cursor over the one at the middle of the bottom and drag it upwards. The chart gets shorter but it becomes squashed and looks wrong.

Press CTRL+Z to restore it. Try dragging the handle in the bottom right corner inwards. The chart shortens and gets narrower in proportion so that its shape is retained. Drag until the chart is about three-quarters of its original size.

> You can drag the handle in the middle of any side to move that side inwards or outwards. Dragging a corner handle moves the two adjacent sides, keeping the overall width and height in proportion.

Click on the column chart below it and drag any of the corner handles inwards until it's the same width as the X-Y chart.

Right-click in the middle of the X-Y chart and click *Format Picture....* A dialogue box opens. Click on the *Layout* tab. Various **wrapping** styles are shown: these control how text on the page will be placed around the chart. Click 🐕 (above *Square*), then click [OK].

> Charts, pictures, drawings and embedded spreadsheets are all classed as graphics. Wrapping controls how text on the page appears around a graphic. The options are:
>
> - *In line with text: the graphic is like a character in the text (rather than being somewhere to the side of it). If the graphic is higher than other characters in the line of text, the spacing of the lines increases to allow it to fit. Small graphics such as* [start] *can be placed in line. A larger graphic can be put in its own paragraph so it sits on the page without any text alongside it.*
>
> - *Square: text fits in alongside the graphic which needs be placed on the left or right side. If you put it in the middle, you'll get text on both sides which isn't normally what you'd want.*
>
> - *Tight: For a picture, this is generally the same as Square. A drawing such as a logo might not be square, e.g. it might be a circle or a triangle. In that case, Tight*

allows the text to follow the actual shape of the drawing rather than its rectangular container.

- *Behind text: Text is placed as if the graphic wasn't there, then the graphic is placed behind it. This can be used to set a light-coloured logo or a word such as DRAFT as a background.*

- *In front of text: Text is placed as if the graphic wasn't there, then the graphic is placed over the text. Text behind it is hidden unless the graphic has transparent areas.*

There are additional options on other tabs in the Format Picture dialogue box. You can set a border and background colour for the graphic.

Right-click on the column chart and click *Format Picture....* Again, set its wrapping on the *Layout* tab to *Square*.

Note the **anchor** symbol (circled above). Put the mouse cursor in the middle of the column chart. It changes to four arrows pointing in different directions. Drag the chart downwards. The anchor moves with it. Drag until the anchor is to the left of *This chart shows the age*.

9.6 Sizing and anchoring graphics 111

Release the left mouse button, then press it again and drag the chart upwards so that the anchor is back alongside *This chart shows the age*. Also drag sideways to align the right hand side of the chart with the right hand margin.

> *This works a bit strangely but the chart is now correctly alongside and anchored to This chart shows the age. The chart will move with it when you make changes to the document.*

Click on the X-Y chart. It also has an anchor symbol. Put the mouse cursor in the middle of the chart. Drag downwards until the anchor symbol is alongside *I compared*. You may also need to move the chart sideways so its left hand side lines up with the left hand margin.

Click to put the text cursor just before *Taller people*. Press RETURN several times until *Taller People* is below the X-Y chart and its line widens out.

> *Notice that the column chart moves down, remaining alongside This chart shows the age.*

Press CTRL+* to hide the non-printing character markers. Page 1 now looks good.

If you right-click on a chart or other graphic and click *Format Picture...*, you'll see [Advanced...] on the *Layout* tab. Click it to open another dialogue box. On its *Picture Position* tab, you can set exactly where the graphic should appear relative to the page or its anchor. You can lock a graphic to a fixed place on the page instead of having it move with text. The *Text Wrapping* tab lets you set additional wrapping options, including whether or not text appears both sides of a centred graphic.

> *When you paste a chart, picture or other graphic, Word sets its wrapping option to In line with text. Options on the Picture Position tab are irrelevant. They are shown in grey (**greyed out**) and you can't change them.*

> *Unfortunately it's often hard to figure out why icons, menu items or options in a dialogue box are greyed out.*

> *Once you've changed the wrapping option, options on the Picture Position tab can be changed.*

What you learned:

- **How to change the size of a chart or other graphic.**

- How to keep the height and width of a graphic in proportion when you resize it.
- How to set the text wrapping option so that text appears alongside a graphic.
- How to anchor a graphic to a specific paragraph so it moves with it when you make changes.
- That you can move a graphic from side to side on the page.
- *What is meant by a "graphic".*
- *What the various options are for how text wraps around a graphic.*
- *How to insert a graphic so it sits in your text just like a character.*
- *That options in a dialogue box are sometimes greyed out and cannot be changed.*
- *That it may not be easy to figure out why an icon, menu item or option is greyed out.*

9.7 Adjusting the embedded spreadsheet

Click below the embedded spreadsheet on page 2, then press LEFT ARROW two or three times so the text cursor is just to the left of the spreadsheet. Type *The 10 people* and press RETURN.

Click on *The 10 people*, select *Heading 1* in the paragraph style selection box and click ☰.

You may have trouble seeing all of the embedded spreadsheet. Click *View > Zoom....* A dialogue box opens. Select *Text width* and click [OK].

> There are other zoom options. For example, you can choose to see the entire page at once but the text will probably be too small to read.

Click on the embedded spreadsheet, then click ☰. Double-click the spreadsheet to open it.

Use the spreadsheet scrollbars (arrowed in the Section 9.3 screenshot) to put the top left cell that needs to be visible in the top left of the window. It's cell *B1* in this case. Adjust the width of the columns if needed so the data in each one is visible without too much extra space. Drag the black square handles (two of them are circled in the screenshot) to resize the window so you can see all the cells that you want to be visible without unwanted blank rows or columns.

> *Remember: you change the width of a spreadsheet column by placing the mouse cursor between the letters at the top and dragging.*

> *The embedded spreadsheet can be any size but only the cells that are visible in the window when it's open will be visible in the document when it's closed.*

Click outside the spreadsheet to close it. Now page 2 is the way we want it.

Close the new document. You won't be using it again but you can save it for posterity if you want. You can also close the *People* spreadsheet, discarding any changes.

What you learned:

- **Another way to zoom to see more or less of the page at a time on the screen.**
- **How to choose which cells in an embedded spreadsheet are visible.**

10 Drawing and Columns

If you need to lay out a magazine or newspaper, you can use a desktop publishing (DTP) program. Microsoft Publisher is a well-known DTP program suitable for everyday use. Scribus is a free open-source program which is quite capable but perhaps not as user-friendly as its commercial rivals. Professional publishers use very powerful and expensive DTP programs.

Word has DTP capabilities too. This chapter shows how to use it to make a simple newsletter. It also uses Word Picture to create and embed a simple logo.

10.1 Setting up columns

Click [start] and go to *My Documents*. Open the *WP files* folder and open *LazyDog* (the Word document you made in Chapter 4).

Press CTRL+A to select all the text and CTRL+C to copy it to the clipboard.

Click at the left hand end of the top toolbar. A new blank Word document opens. Press CTRL+V. The drivel about the fox and the dog is pasted into it.

Drag over the first three paragraphs of text to select them. Click . A small box appears showing four columns of text. Place the mouse cursor over the second one from the left. It and the leftmost one become highlighted. Click. The selected text is now in two columns. Click to fully justify it.

Click on the **drawing toolbar** below the document. A box may appear in the document saying *Create your drawing here*. Ignore it, move the mouse cursor to the left margin anywhere outside the box and hold down the left mouse button. Drag horizontally to the right margin. A line appears. Make sure it's horizontal, then release the mouse button.

> *Holding down SHIFT while you drag limits the angles that the line can have. This makes it a bit easier to make it horizontal.*

> *Office toolbars can be enabled or disabled. If you don't see the drawing toolbar, click View > Toolbars > Drawing.*

> *The Create your drawing here box is a feature called Drawing canvas. You can use it to make a drawing such as a flowchart that's easier to modify. Many people find it annoying although it disappears as soon as you start drawing outside it. You can turn the feature off by clicking Tools > Options, clicking on the General tab and clearing the tickbox next to Automatically create drawing canvas when inserting AutoShapes.*

Place the mouse cursor over the line so that it changes to four arrows pointing in different directions. Drag the line up or down so it's between the bottom of the two columns of text and the line starting *What do these dogs like*.

With the mouse cursor still over the line, right-click and select *Format AutoShape...*. A dialogue box appears. Click on the *Colors and Lines* tab. Under *Line*, set *Weight* to *1.5 pt*. Click [OK].

> *Word has many more drawing tools on the bottom toolbar that you can experiment with.*

What you learned:

- **That you can start a new document by clicking** 📄.
- **How to put selected text in columns.**
- **How to draw, position and format a separator line.**
- *How to enable and disable toolbars.*
- *What the drawing canvas is and that you can ignore or disable it.*

10.2 Making a logo

> *This uses the drawing tools to create a new logo. If you already had a logo as a file on your computer, you could use Insert > Picture > From File... as discussed in Section 9.4.*

> *Computers work with two different types of pictures and drawings. A **bit-mapped** picture specifies the brightness and colour of each point in it. It can show anything: photographs are always bit-mapped. If you try to enlarge a bit-map too much, its individual points become visible as squares and it looks bad.*

> *A **vector graphic** contains instructions to draw shapes, colour them in and overlay them. It's limited in what it can show but*

has the advantage that you can easily move and change individual shapes and you can enlarge the graphic to any size.

Paint works with bit-mapped pictures. The Word drawing tools you'll use here create vector graphics.

Click before the first paragraph to place the text cursor there. Click *Insert > Object....* A dialogue box opens. Scroll down in the *Object type:* list to find *Microsoft Word Picture.* Double-click on it A blank drawing appears. The menus and toolbars change to those needed to work on the drawing.

You could have clicked once on Microsoft Word Picture to select it, then clicked [OK] *but in many situations, including this one, you can save time by double-clicking on the option you want in a dialogue box.*

There's a square on the blank drawing which represents the area that will be visible in your document. You can ignore this for now.

You already drew a line without inserting a Word Picture. You could draw the logo the same way but there would be some problems setting the text wrapping and copying it elsewhere.

There are other things you can do with Insert > Object.... You can insert a new Excel spreadsheet and, of course, this can look like a list or table in the document. This could be handy if, for example, you're preparing an invoice. Let the spreadsheet do the arithmetic.

You can click Insert > Object and click on the Create from File tab in the dialogue box to embed an existing file. This makes a copy of it that becomes part of the document and is saved in its file.

If you tick the Link to file tickbox, your document is linked to the specified file instead of containing a copy of it. The document updates automatically when the linked file changes. For example you could record sales in a spreadsheet and prepare several different reports linked to its file. Updating the spreadsheet updates all the reports too but if you e-mail a report file to someone else, you need to send the spreadsheet file as well.

Click ◢ on the drawing toolbar at the bottom. The *WordArt Gallery* window opens. Double click on **WordArt** in the top row. The *Edit WordArt Text* window opens with *Your Text Here* highlighted. Type *Sunnyside News* (which automatically replaces the highlighted text) and click [OK].

> *WordArt makes it easy to show words with various special effects. We're using it to form words into a semicircle. You can look at the picture later on to see the effect we want to create.*

Move the mouse cursor over *Sunnyside News* and click. A box appears around it with eight small black squares. These are handles. Drag the middle handle below *Sunnyside News* downwards. A dashed line appears representing the curve of the words. Continue dragging until the line forms a semicircle.

Right-click and click *Format WordArt....* The *Format WordArt* dialogue box appears. Click on the *Layout* tab, then double-click [icon] (above *Behind text*). *Sunnyside News* is now surrounded by small circles. These are also handles.

> *The black square handles indicated that the WordArt object had the In line with text wrapping style. Now that you've changed this, the handles have changed to circles and you can move and group the object.*

Press CTRL+C to copy the WordArt to the clipboard, then press CTRL+V to add a second copy.

Right-click on the second copy and click on *Format WordArt....* The dialogue box appears. Click on the *Size* tab. In the *Scale* section, click to tick the *Lock aspect ratio* box, then change the *Height* box from *100%* to *105%*.

Click on the *Colors and Lines* tab, change the *Fill Color* to *Grey-40%* and the *Line Color* to *No Line*. Click [OK].

> *Vector graphic shapes have a **fill** and a **stroke**. The fill is the colour inside the shape while the stroke is the line around it. You've set the fill to Grey and made the stroke (line) invisible. Sometimes you may want to set the fill to none and just use the stroke. Sometimes, you'll want to use both.*

> *When you're changing the fill colour and you move the mouse cursor over a possible colour, you'll see a tooltip naming it.*

While holding down ALT, drag the grey copy until its dashed line is centred over the black copy. Release the mouse button.

> *Unless you hold down ALT, you can only drag in fixed steps. This is often helpful when you want to keep things aligned but, in this case, it prevents you from putting the copy in the exact place you want.*

We're aiming to have *Sunnyside News* in black with the larger grey copy behind it as a shadow but you'll probably have the grey copy on top. If so, right-click on it, and click on *Order > Send to Back*.

> *If you have more than two overlapping objects, you can use Order > Bring Forward and Order > Send Backward to stack them in front of one another in any order you want.*

> *When you set the colour of an object, you can also choose to make it partly transparent so that objects behind it can be seen dimly.*

You should have one set of handles around *Sunnyside News*. Hold down SHIFT and click on the black copy. There should now be two sets of handles indicating that both the black and grey copies are selected. If there is still only one set, hold down SHIFT and click on the grey copy.

Right-click on either copy and click *Grouping > Group*. The two copies are now **grouped** with just one set of handles. You can easily move or resize them together. Try moving them a bit.

Click ◯ on the bottom toolbar. Place the mouse cursor at the centre of the arc of *Sunnyside News*. Hold down SHIFT and CTRL, then drag outwards. A circle appears and grows larger. Stop dragging when it is the right size to fit inside *Sunnyside News*. Release SHIFT and CTRL.

> *Holding down SHIFT ensures that you draw a circle (with the same height and width) rather than an ellipse. Holding down CTRL ensures that the circle is centred at the point where you started dragging outwards.*

Double-click on the circle. The *Format AutoShape* dialogue box appears. Click on the *Colors and Lines* tab. Under *Fill*, set *Color* to *Yellow*. Under *Line*, set *Color* to *No Line*. Click [OK].

> *As you saw earlier, you can open the Format AutoShape dialogue box by right-clicking on a shape and choosing Format AutoShape... but double-clicking is quicker.*

Hold down ALT and drag the circle so it fits correctly in the arc of *Sunnyside News*. The logo is now complete.

There should be a small floating *Edit Picture* toolbar. Click ▣. This automatically resizes the area that will be visible in your document. Click Close Picture.

Click on the logo in your document. It's now enclosed in a square with eight black square handles. Drag the top slider at the left hand end of the ruler leftwards to line up the logo's left side with the margin. Drag the handle at the bottom right corner inwards until the logo is the correct size.

> *You could now click on the logo and use copy and paste to copy it to another Word document.*

What you learned:

- How to insert a Word Picture.
- How to use WordArt to put text on a curve.
- How to create a copy of the text, enlarge it and change its colour.
- How to put the copy behind the original text to create a shadow effect.
- How to select multiple objects and group them.
- How to draw a circle and change its colour.
- How to select which part of the Word Picture is visible in the document.
- *The differences between bit-mapped and vector graphics.*
- *That you can insert a new spreadsheet into a Word document.*
- *That you can insert a copy of an existing file such as a spreadsheet.*
- *That you can link to an existing file so that changes to it automatically appear in your document.*
- *How to change the stacking order of objects and use transparency.*
- *How to use ALT, CTRL and SHIFT when drawing.*
- *What Fill and Stroke (Line) are.*
- *That, once you've made a logo, you can copy and paste it to other documents.*

10.3 Adding a text box

Click away from the logo to deselect it. Make sure no text is selected. Click *Insert > Text Box*. Again, you might see the *Create your drawing here* box which you can ignore. Drag to create a box across the bottom of the yellow circle in the logo. Select *Arial* in the typeface selector box and *22* point as the font size. Click ≡, then type *September 2011*.

Position the mouse cursor over the edge of the text box and double-click. The *Format Text Box* dialogue box appears. Click the *Colors and Lines* tab. Under *Fill*, set *Color* to *Bright Green*. Click OK .

Drag the middle handle at the bottom of the text box to adjust its height so *September 2011* just fits nicely. Position the mouse cursor over the box edge away from the handles and drag the whole box so its bottom edge lines up with the bottom of the yellow circle.

September 2011

The quick brown fox jumps over a lazy dog. **The quick brown fox jumps over the lazy dog.** *The quick brown fox jumps over a lazy dog.* The quick brown fox jumps over the lazy dog. ***The quick brown fox jumps over the lazy dog.***

The quick brown fox jumps over a lazy dog. **The quick brown fox jumps over the**

lazy dog. *The quick brown fox jumps over a lazy dog.* The quick brown fox jumps over the lazy dog. ***The quick brown fox jumps over the lazy dog.***

THE QUICK BROWN FOX JUMPS OVER A LAZY DOG. **The quick brown fox jumps over the lazy dog.** *The quick brown fox jumps over a lazy dog.* The quick brown fox jumps over the lazy dog. ***The quick brown fox jumps over the lazy dog.***

What do these dogs like?	Walkies	Chasing things
	Barking	Eating Sleeping

If you need to delete a text box, click on its edge so that the handles appear, then press DELETE.

Close the new document. You won't be using it again but you can save it for posterity if you want.

What you learned:

- **How to create a text box.**
- **That you can type text into a text box and format it.**
- **How to change the colour of a text box.**

- How to resize and move a text box.
- *What happens when objects overlap.*
- *How to use transparency and the different Order options.*
- *How to delete a text box.*

10.4 Making a letterhead

Now that you've seen how to import or create graphics and set up text boxes, you can design your own letterhead.

You can put a logo at the top. Perhaps you already have one that you can insert as a picture or graphic or you could design one with Word Picture.

You can put contact details, perhaps in a text box, at the top or bottom of the page.

When you're happy with the design, save it as a Word template (Section 6.10). No need to have the letterhead printed, just open the template whenever you start writing a letter.

> *You need to weigh up the advantages and disadvantages of doing this. A letterhead printed with each letter will print more slowly, will probably be lower quality and may cost more in ink or toner. On the other hand, you'll be sure your letters line up with the letterhead, you won't have to change paper in the printer, there won't be a minimum print run and you can change details on the letterhead (e.g. your phone number) at any time.*

11 Mail merge

Mail merge is a word-processor feature that you can use to print personalised versions of a standard letter for people whose names and addresses are in a list somewhere on the computer. You'll have received many of these letters yourself.

Mail merge is an advanced feature but this book covers it since small businesses and organisations will often want to use it.

Before you do a mail-merge, you need to do some planning:

- Where are the names and addresses? Can you get them into Excel or export them as a file that Word can use?

  You saw in Chapter 8 how tedious it is to type a lot of names and addresses. If the names and addresses are in a database, they can probably be exported as a CSV file, perhaps by the database administrator.

- Do you want to send the letter to everyone in the list? If not, is there information in the list itself that can be used to identify who should get a letter?

- Do you want to use windowed envelopes, sticky address labels or print the addresses directly onto envelopes?

  You can buy address labels and run them through the printer. Printing directly onto envelopes can involve a lot of trial and error. Windowed envelopes are easiest and the addresses and letters can't get out of step.

- Will you use pre-printed letterhead paper, a letterhead template or just plain paper?

- Do you have a scanned version of the signature you want to use?

  It's worth making one so you don't have to sign the letters individually by hand. The procedure depends on your scanner – look at its instructions.

- What do you want the letter to say?

11.1 Making the address list

Click [start], go to *My Documents* and open *People.xls* (the spreadsheet you made in Chapter 8).

Click *File > Save As....* The *Save As...* dialogue box opens. In *Save as type*, select *CSV (Comma delimited) (*.csv)*. Click [Save]. You may need to click [OK] to save the active sheet and [Yes] to confirm that you don't mind omitting the formatting and charts. The address list is saved in *My Documents* as *People.csv*. Close *People.xls*.

> Almost all database programs can export CSV (**Comma-Separated-Values**) *files although how to do that is outside the scope of this book. As you'll see later, you can get the addresses directly from the spreadsheet or from an Access database but now that the addresses are in a CSV file, you can use the same procedure wherever they came from.*
>
> *If you're interested, go to My Documents, right-click on People.csv, choose Open With and click Choose Program.... A list of installed programs appears. Click on Notepad to choose it and click* [OK]. *The file opens in the Notepad program: it's as if the list was on paper tape and you'd printed it. You'll see how simple it is. Data for the columns is separated with commas. The first line gives the column headings.*
>
> *You can't just click on People.csv to view it: the csv extension is probably associated with Excel, not Notepad (Section 5.2).*
>
> *If you have a CSV file from another source such as a database, you can start the procedure with the next section.*

What you learned:

- **How to export the addresses in the Excel spreadsheet as a CSV file.**
- *What a CSV (Comma-Separated-Values) file is.*
- *That addresses in other databases can be exported as a CSV file too.*
- *How to open a file with a program other than the one it's associated with.*
- *How to view a simple text file using Notepad.*
- *That you can import addresses in a spreadsheet directly.*

11.2 Making a template letter

Start a new Word document or open your letterhead template.

Click *Tools > Letters and Mailings > Mail Merge...*. The **Mail Merge wizard** starts in the task pane to the right of the document.

Check that the *Letters* radio button is selected. At the bottom of the pane, click *Next: Starting document*.

Check that the *Use the current document* radio button is selected. At the bottom of the pane, click *Next: Select recipients*.

Check that the *Use an existing list* radio button is selected. In the middle of the pane, click *Browse...*. The *Select Data Source* box opens.

Click *My Documents* on the left side of the box. Find *People.csv* (its *Type* shows as *Microsoft Excel Comma Separated Values File*) and double-click on it.

> *You may notice that the People.xls spreadsheet is shown too (its Type is Microsoft Excel Worksheet). When the data is in a spreadsheet, you can select that and use it directly. You can also get the data directly from some types of database (e.g. Access) but using a CSV file will almost always work.*

The *Mail Merge Recipients* box opens showing a list of the names in the file. Click [OK], then click *Next: Write your letter* at the bottom of the task pane.

> *We'll be using the Mail Merge Recipients box in Section 11.3.*

Press RETURN until the text cursor is about 5.5 cm (2.2 inches) from the top of the page.

> *This distance might not be right for the envelopes you'll use. You can measure the position of the window or measure the position of the address on an existing letter that fits correctly and use those measurements instead.*

Click *Address block...* in the middle of the task pane. The *Insert Address Block* dialogue box opens. Click [Match Fields...].

Word expects to find particular information in the address list such as the recipients' first and last names. It's quite smart at guessing which fields in the list to use but it doesn't always get it right. In this case, you'll probably see that it hasn't managed to identify which field contains the City name. Click ▼ next to *(not matched)* alongside *City* and choose *Town* from the list that appears. Check that the other fields are matched correctly.

> *You'll see that other information such as State also shows (not matched). That's OK, the information isn't in our list anyway.*

Click [OK]. Review the other options in the *Insert Address Block* box. They're reasonably self-explanatory. When you're happy with them, click [OK].

> *Word uses Mr. Randall as an example, he's not in our address list.*

<<AddressBlock>> appears as a marker in the document showing where the address will be. Press RETURN several times, then click *Insert > Date and Time....* Click on the format you want to use for the date of the letter so it's highlighted. Click to tick the *Update automatically* tickbox, then click [OK].

> *Today's date appears in the document. Because you ticked Update automatically, this will automatically change to the date when you actually print the letters.*

> *You can use Insert > Date and Time whenever you want to put the current date in a document. Often you won't want to tick Update automatically. For example, if you write a letter to someone and keep a copy on your computer, you'll want the date to always match that on the letter that you printed and sent off.*

Press RETURN three times. Click *Greeting line...* in the middle of the task pane. The *Greeting Line* dialogue box opens. It's also reasonably self-explanatory. Choose the form you want for the name (e.g. *Mr. Randall*) and click [OK].

Press RETURN several times. Type *Yours sincerely* and press RETURN.

If you have a scanned signature, click *Insert > Picture > From File...* and choose its file. Click on the inserted signature and drag its handles to make it the right size. You may want to type your name on another line below it.

If you don't have a scanned signature, put enough blank lines below *Yours sincerely* to make room for your signature, then type your name.

At the bottom of the task pane, click *Next: Preview your letters*. You see the letter with <<AddressBlock>> and <<GreetingLine>> replaced with the details for one of the names in the list filled in.

11.2 Making a template letter   **127**

Check that the letter looks OK.

> *You can step through the names in the list by clicking* `>>` *and* `<<` *near the top of the task pane.*

Click *File > Print...* and print one of the letters. Fold the letter and try it in a windowed envelope (if you're planning to use these). Confirm that the address shows in the window, that the date line is comfortably below the window and that the signature spacing is OK. If there are problems, add or delete blank lines and/or change the left margin, then print and recheck the letter.

Click *File > Save As....* Choose *Document Template (*.dot)* as the type and type a suitable name (e.g. *FormLetter*) as the *File name*. Click `Save`, then close Word.

> *For a one-off letter, you can work through the wizard from start to end but it's handy to have a template with the signature set up and the address block and date in the right places.*

What you learned:

- **How to start the Mail Merge wizard.**
- **How to specify the address list to be used.**
- **How to insert the address block and line it up with the envelope window.**
- **How to match fields so that the addresses are shown correctly.**
- **How to insert the date into your document and change its format.**
- **How to insert the greeting line into your letter.**
- **How to include your signature in the letter so you don't have to sign every copy.**
- *That you can have an inserted date stay fixed or have it update automatically.*

11.3 Sending a form letter

Start Word and click *File > New....* In the *New Document* task pane on the right, click *On my computer....* Click the *General* tab in the dialogue box and double-click the *FormLetter* template. You may see messages that SQL commands will run. Click `Yes`.

> *Word re-reads the file containing the address list. If the file containing the list has changed, the changes will be present in the new letter. If you used a CSV file, you or the database administrator will need to export it again and you'll need to reopen the template so that the letter reflects any recent changes to the database.*

Click *Tools > Letters and Mailings > Mail Merge...* to start the Mail Merge wizard in the task pane to the right of the document.

At the bottom of the pane, check which step is showing. Click *Next:* or *Previous:* if necessary to reach *Step 3* of the wizard.

> *You specified the address list file and matched the fields when you created the template. This information was stored in the template file but you can change it now if you need to use a different list. In the middle of the task pane, click on Select a different list... and choose the list file as before.*

In the middle of the task pane, click on *Edit recipient list....* The *Mail Merge Recipients* box opens, showing all the names in the list. There's a tick box next to each name.

There might be some blank entries in the list. Click ▼ next to the *Surname* heading and click on *(Nonblanks)* to exclude them.

We don't want to send the letter to everyone in the list. We're going to omit anyone 65 or older or with a BMI of 30 or more. There are two ways we can do this.

The first way is simple to understand. Click [Select All] so that all the names are ticked. Scroll to the right to see the *Age* column. Click on its heading so that the names are sorted by age in increasing order.

Find the first line where the age is 65 or more and click on it so it's highlighted. Scroll to the left. Clear the tickbox on the highlighted line and on each line lower down.

Scroll to the right to see the *BMI* column. Click on its heading so that the names are sorted by BMI in increasing order.

Find the first line where the BMI is 30 or more and click on it so it's highlighted. Scroll to the left. Clear any tickboxes that are still ticked on the highlighted line and lines lower down. Only four names should still be ticked. These people would get the letter.

Now we'll try the second method which is much quicker and easier if there are hundreds of names in the list. Click [Select All] so all the names are ticked again.

Click ▼ next to any of the headings (e.g. *Surname*) and click on *(Advanced...)* in the list that appears. The **Query Options** dialogue box opens.

Click on the *Filter Records* tab. In the first row, choose *Age* from the *Field:* drop-down list, choose *Less than* from the *Comparison:* list and enter *65* in the *Compare to:* box.

> *If you clicked (Nonblanks) earlier, this condition will already be set in the first row. Make sure the first box of the second row says And, then enter Age, Less than and 65 in that row.*

In the next row, make sure the first box says *And*. Choose *BMI* from *Field:* and *Less than* from *Comparison:*. Enter *30* in the *Compare to:* box. Click [OK]. Now, you only see the same four names that were ticked before.

> *To remove a filter so all the names reappear, open the Query Options dialogue box, click [Clear All] then click [OK].*

> *If you want the letters to be printed in a particular order, e.g. sorted by postcode, either click on the column heading or use the Sort Records tab in the Query Options box.*

Click [OK] to close the *Mail Merge Recipients* box. At the bottom of the task pane, click *Next: Write your letter*.

If you changed the address list file from the one in the template, you need to review the field matching again. Click *More items...* in the middle of the task pane. The *Insert Merge Field* dialogue box opens. Click [Match Fields...], adjust the field matching as before and click [OK]. Click [Cancel] to close the *Insert Merge Field* box.

In the document, click below *<<GreetingLine>>* and type (pressing RETURN when you see ¶):

> *Now that you're years old, perhaps you're thinking about life insurance.*¶
> ¶
> *I can offer you a choice of excellent policies. Please give me a call.*
> ¶

Click before *years* and click *More items...* in the task pane. The *Insert Merge Field* dialogue box opens. Make sure the *Database Fields* radio button is selected. Double-click on *Age* in the *Fields:* list. Click

[Close] to close the dialogue box.

Make sure there's a space before and after <<*Age*>> in the letter. Adjust the rest of the letter so it looks nice.

«AddressBlock»

Thursday, 15 September 2011

«GreetingLine»

Now that you're «Age» years old, perhaps you're thinking about life insurance.

I can offer you a choice of excellent policies. Please give me a call.

Yours sincerely

John Smith

At the bottom of the task pane, click *Next: Preview your letters*. As when you made the letter template in Section 11.2, you can check that the letters look correct. You'll see that each person's age is shown. Click *Next: Complete the merge* at the bottom of the task pane.

You now have two choices. You can click on *Print...* in the middle of the task pane and print the letters right away. Make sure the radio button next to *All* is selected in the first dialogue box and click [OK]. Choose the printer and options in the next dialogue box and click [OK].

Alternatively, you can click *Edit individual letters...* in the middle of the task pane. Make sure the radio button next to *All* is selected in the dialogue box and click [OK]. Word creates a new document containing all the letters, each one starting on a new page. You can check the letters and make changes to personalise individual ones before printing the whole document as in Section 4.14. Close the document containing the individual letters, saving it first if you want to.

Save the form letter document if you think you might want to use it (not just the template) again. If you're using window envelopes, you can close the document.

If you're using address labels or printing the addresses on envelopes, click *Previous* at the bottom of the task pane until you reach *Step 1* of the wizard. Continue as described in Section 11.4 for envelopes or 11.5 for labels.

> *If you're not using a scanned signature, remember to sign the letters. If you're not using window envelopes, be sure to put the letters in the right envelopes.*

What you learned:

- **How to make a new form letter using the template.**
- **That you can select a different address list.**
- **How to match fields if you're using a different list.**
- **Two ways to select recipients so only those meeting certain criteria get the letter.**
- **How to insert fields from the address list into the body of the letter itself.**
- **How to print the form letters directly to the printer.**
- **How to put the letters in a new document where you can review and personalise them before printing.**
- *That, if the database was created directly from a spreadsheet, it will stay up to date.*
- *That, if the database was created from a CSV file, the file should be updated.*
- *How to print the letters in a particular order.*
- *How to remove a filter.*

11.4 Printing Envelopes

With your form letter document open and the *Mail Merge* task pane at *Step 1*, click to select the *Envelopes* radio button. Click *Next: Starting document* at the bottom of the pane.

Make sure the *Change document layout* radio button is checked and click on *Envelope options...* in the middle of the task pane. A dialogue box opens.

Click on the *Envelope Options* tab and choose your envelope size from the drop down list. Click on the *Printing Options* tab and click on the picture showing how you'll feed envelopes into the printer. Be sure to select whether the envelopes are fed face up or face down and whether they will be fed individually (*SSF* – Single Sheet Feed) or from a paper tray. Click [OK] and [OK] again in the confirmation box that appears.

The form letter itself is deleted and replaced with a blank page the size of the envelope. At the bottom of the task pane, click *Next: Select recipients*, then click *Next: Arrange your envelope*.

> *The envelopes need to match the letters you printed earlier. You don't want to make any changes to the recipient list or its sort order.*

If you want a return address on the envelopes, type it now, being sure to press RETURN afterwards.

In the middle of the task pane, click on *Address block....* The *Insert Address Block* box appears. Check its options, then click [OK]. <<AddressBlock>> is added to the blank envelope. Place the text cursor before it, adjust the left margin and press RETURN repeatedly until the block is at a suitable position on the envelope.

At the bottom of the task pane, click *Next: Preview your envelopes*. As with the letters, you can check the envelopes. Make any needed changes to the fonts and address block position, then click *Next: Complete the merge* at the bottom of the pane.

Click *Print...* in the middle of the pane, choose *All* and set the print options. You may need to load the envelopes into the printer before printing or feed them individually while printing.

> *As with the letters, you can choose to create a new document containing all the envelopes but this isn't likely to be useful.*

> *Take care to stack the letters and the envelopes in the order they are printed. This makes it much easier to match them up.*

Close the document, being sure to discard the changes. You don't want to overwrite the letters themselves.

> You can save a template for envelopes but it might not be much use. You'd need to be very careful to choose the right recipient list and set up the filter and sort order to match a new letter.

11.5 Printing Labels

With your form letter document open and the *Mail Merge* task pane at *Step 1*, click to select the *Labels* radio button. Click *Next: Starting document* at the bottom of the pane.

Make sure the *Change document layout* radio button is checked and click on *Label options...* in the middle of the task pane. A dialogue box opens.

Click on the radio button for your printer type: *Dot matrix* (tractor fed labels) or *Laser/ink jet* (sheet fed labels). Word knows the dimensions for many commercial labels. Choose the label manufacturer and click to highlight the label type.

> If your labels aren't listed, you can click [New Label...] and enter the dimensions. These may need trial and error.

Click [OK] and [OK] again in the confirmation box that appears. The form letter itself is deleted and replaced with a page of blank labels. At the bottom of the task pane, click *Next: Select recipients*, then click *Next: Arrange your labels*.

> The labels need to match the letters you printed earlier. You don't want to make any changes to the recipient list or its sort order.

In the middle of the task pane, click on *Address block...*. The *Insert Address Block* box appears. Check its options, then click [OK]. <<AddressBlock>> is added to the first blank label. Place the text cursor before it and adjust the left margin so that the block is at a suitable position on the label.

At the bottom of the task pane, click *Next: Preview your labels*. As with the letters, you can check the first label on the sheet. Make any needed changes to the margin and font, then click *Previous: Arrange your labels* at the bottom of the pane.

Click [Update all labels] on the task pane. The remaining blank labels on the sheet are filled in.

> *With form letters and envelopes, a copy of the document is printed for each recipient. Labels are different: each page contains multiple labels. <<Next Record>> tells Word to progress to the next recipient in the list.*

Click *Next: Preview your labels* at the bottom of the task pane. Check that the labels look correct.

Click *Next: Complete the merge* at the bottom of the pane.

Click *Print...* in the middle of the pane, choose *All* and set the print options. You may need to load the label sheets into the printer paper tray before printing or feed them individually while printing.

> *As with the letters, you can choose to create a new document containing all the labels but this isn't likely to be useful.*

> *Take care to stack the letters and the sheets of labels in the order they are printed. This makes it much easier to match them up.*

Close the document, being sure to discard the changes. You don't want to overwrite the letters themselves.

> *You can save a template for labels but it might not be much use. You'd need to be very careful to choose the right recipient list and set up the filter and sort order to match a new letter.*

12 Epilogue

I hope you've found this book to be clear, informative, useful and not too overwhelming or intimidating.

Next time you need to do something, you may remember that Microsoft Office can do it but not remember how. Check the index.

There are many features of Word that the book hasn't covered. For example, you might want to format some paragraphs with a *drop capital* – a large letter at the start. Help shows how to do that.

There are many more features of Word Picture and Excel spreadsheets left for you to discover too.

Although web browsing is only covered very briefly and e-mail not at all, you'll have picked up enough conventions and jargon to have a good chance of figuring these out yourself.

Sometimes you'll think *Wouldn't it be useful if Windows / Word / Excel / the computer could do such and such?* It probably can. Try the Help menu or a search engine.

Of course the computer's not magic - it's not going to write a best-selling novel for you. Remember that the most important thing about anything you write isn't what it looks like. **It's what it says.**

> *Just type and type, leaving all the formatting until you're happy with what you've written.*

> *Could the order be improved? Don't retype, use cut and paste.*

> *Make full use of features such as paragraph styles, cross-references, automatic numbering and table of contents.*

> *You'll be much more willing to make changes when Word can renumber everything and you haven't invested too much time faffing about choosing fonts, etc. Leave all that to the end.*

> *You can't do that with a typewriter: that's the beauty of a word processor.*

Alphabetical Index

application (app)...11
ASCII (American Standards Committee for Information Interchange). 5
binary digit (bit)...5
BIOS...10
break...
    line...37
    page...**37,** 72
button..17
byte...5
chapter..
    number..**72,** 78
character...5
    colour..68
    font..41
    foreign..44
    non-printing..45
    size..40
    style..39
    subscript..68
    superscript...68
    symbol..44
    typeface...40
    underline..**39,** 68
clipboard...66
    copy...25, **33,** 62
    cut...**33,** 62, 136
    paste...**26,** 62, 83, 102, 105, 136
    paste formatted text...105
    paste special...104
    paste unformatted text...105
computer..
    boot...10
    hibernate...21
    restart...21
    stand by..21
CPU (Central Processing Unit)..6
crash..8
cursor..14

- mouse..14
- text..24, **28**
- data...5, 6, 8, 9, 59
  - sort...99
- data stick..12
- database..124
- date...96, 127
- desktop...**18,** 62
- dialogue box..29
- document...7, 9, 16, 22, 56
  - author...77
  - meta-data..77
  - word count..78
- drawing...117
- drop-down menu..27
- DTP (desktop publishing)..115
- e-mail..53, 61
- embed...
  - spreadsheet..117
- equation..109
- field...**78,** 130
- file...51, 56
  - associate..59
  - attach to e-mail..53, 61
  - copy..60
  - CSV (Comma Separated Values)..............................**125,** 129
  - date..58
  - directory..56
  - hidden..80
  - list..58
  - name...56
  - recently used..101
  - recover...**51,** 63
  - save..**50,** 91
  - save as..51, 79
  - shortcut..62
  - sort...58
  - template..**80,** 123, 128, 134, 135
  - type..59
- find and replace...29
  - all...30
  - match case..30
  - whole words only..31

floppy disks..50
folder...55
    backup..64
    Desktop...**56,** 63
    Documents and Settings......................................56
    My Documents...........................54, **56,** 57, 63, 64
    personal..56
    root..56
    temporary..54
font..
    Arial...40
    Courier..41
    mono-spaced...41
    points..40
    proportional..41
    sans-serif...40
    serif...40
    Times New Roman...40
    Webdings..44
    Wingdings...44
giga..**5,** 10
grammar..49
graphic..110
    adaptor..6, 12
    anchor..111
    bit-mapped..116
    border...111
    fill..118
    group..119
    handles..110
    stroke..118
    vector...116
    wrap...110
greyed out..112
hard disk...9, 55, 60
    external..65
help menu..**84,** 136
highlight...25
icon...**26**
justification..
    centre..38
    full..38
    left...37

right..37
keyboard..6, 12
    ALT..**17,** 101, 107
    arrow..**17,** 28
    BACKSPACE...**17,** 29
    CAPS LOCK...42
    CTRL..**17,** 26, 46, 62, 85, 119
    DELETE..**17,** 28, 122
    ESC..17
    function keys...77
    INSERT..28
    Print Scrn..107
    RETURN..**17,** 34, 37, 45, 82
    SHIFT..**17,** 62, 82, 85, 87, 119
    shortcut...**25**
    SPACEBAR..4, **17**
    TAB..**17,** 35, 45, 74, 82, 101
keylogger...9
kilo...5
laptop..6, 21
letter..124
    address labels..134
    envelope...126, **132**
    filter...130
    letterhead...**123,** 126
    mail merge..124
    print..131
    signature...127
    template..126
link..17
malware..8
mega..5
memory..6, 9
    RAM..9
    ROM..10
motherboard..6
mouse..6, 12, 14
    click...**14,** 16, 17, 28, 55
    cursor......................................**14,** 28, 29, 39, 46, 55, 83, 86, 94, 110
    double-click..**14,** 33, 55, 117
    drag...**14,** 19, 24, 36, 46, 60, 62, 86, 111
    right-click..................................**14,** 48, 58, 71, 94, 110, 125
My Computer..55

object 105
    embed 105
    handle 113
    link 106, **117**
open-source **11,** 108, 115
operating system 11
    Apple 11
    Linux 11
    Microsoft Windows 11
    Ubuntu 11
page ....
    footer 78
    header 78
    landscape 103
    margin 35
    number 78
    portrait 103
    size 103
    tiling 103
paper tape 3
paragraph ....
    bulleting 70
    chapter 71
    indent 35
    margin 35
    numbering 68
    outdent 35
    spacing 34
    style 70
PC (Personal Computer) 13
picture 108
printer 12, **52,** 60, 133, 134
    collate 53
    default 53
    driver 103
    error 103
program 7, 10, 16, 59
    Adobe Photoshop 108
    anti-virus 9
    close 17
    GIMP 108
    LibreOffice .... **vi,** 11, 20, 74
    Microsoft Excel .... vi, **82**

Microsoft Notepad... 74, 125
Microsoft Office...vi, 20
Microsoft Paint... **107,** 117
Microsoft Publisher...115
Microsoft Word... vi, **22,** 74
Microsoft WordPad... 11, 74
multitasking... **18,** 101
OpenOffice...vi
Scribus..115
version..85
radio button...42
Recycle Bin..63
redo...31
ruler..34
screenshot.. v, **15,** 35, 40, 107
search engine... 16, 136
Bing..17
Google...16
select... 25, 33
all..33
extend..33
hover...55
icon...55
spreadsheet cells..85
selector box..39
smartphone...11
source code...11
spelling..48
dictionaries..49
spreadsheet..82
algebraic conventions..88
cell...82
cell range...84
chart.. **94,** 98, 101
column... **82,** 86, 105
currency...89
date and time..97
embed...104
formula... **83,** 95
function...84
percentage...88
reference... **83,** 86, 87
rounding.. 89, 96, 97

row..**82,** 85, 106
    sort..99
    text..**83,** 97
tab stop..**35,** 78
table..74, 102
    delete..108
    of contents..76
    update..77
task pane..**24,** 126
taskbar..18
teleprinter..3
tera...6
text...24
    auto-correction..67
    capitals..42
    overwrite..28
text box...121
    delete..122
thumbdrive..10, **12,** 61, 64
    safely remove..60
tickbox..30
toolbar..26
    drawing..115
    enable..115
tooltip..39
touchpad..6, **14**
typewriter..3, 41, 136
undo...31
updates..11
USB (Universal Serial Bus)..........................60
virus...8
window..16
    close..17
    drag..19
    maximise..18
    minimise..18
    resize...19
    scroll bar...19
    titlebar...16
Windows Vista....................................vi, 56, 59, 65
Windows XP......................................vi, 16, 23, 63
wizard...**81,** 94, 126, 129
word-wrap..37

zoom..**24,** 113

www.ingramcontent.com/pod-product-compliance
Lightning Source LLC
Chambersburg PA
CBHW030749180526
45163CB00003B/960